A
Pocket
GUIDE

TO FORMAL
Logic

KARL LADEROUTE

broadview press

·BROADVIEW PRESS— www.broadviewpress.com
Peterborough, Ontario, Canada

Founded in 1985, Broadview Press remains a wholly independent publishing house. Broadview's focus is on academic publishing; our titles are accessible to university and college students as well as scholars and general readers. With over 800 titles in print, Broadview has become a leading international publisher in the humanities, with world-wide distribution. Broadview is committed to environmentally responsible publishing and fair business practices.

© 2023 Karl Laderoute

Library and Archives Canada Cataloguing in Publication

Title: A pocket guide to formal logic / Karl Laderoute.
Names: Laderoute, Karl, author.
Identifiers: Canadiana (print) 2022042926X | Canadiana (ebook) 20220429286 | ISBN 9781554814701 (softcover) | ISBN 9781770488687 (PDF) | ISBN 9781460408049 (EPUB)
Subjects: LCSH: Logic.
Classification: LCC BC71 .L33 2022 | DDC 160—dc23

Broadview Press handles its own distribution in North America:
PO Box 1243, Peterborough, Ontario K9J 7H5, Canada
555 Riverwalk Parkway, Tonawanda, NY 14150, USA
Tel: (705) 743-8990; Fax: (705) 743-8353
email: customerservice@broadviewpress.com

For all territories outside of North America, distribution is handled by Eurospan Group.

Broadview Press acknowledges the financial support of the Government of Canada for our publishing activities.

Edited by Robert M. Martin
Book design by Michel Vrana

PRINTED IN CANADA

This book is made of paper from well-managed FSC® - certified forests, recycled materials, and other controlled sources.

Contents

Preface for the Student

This book is designed to equip you with the basic tools of formal logic. Formal logic is a branch of logic that utilizes **symbols**. We will use two kinds of symbols. First there are letters (such as P, Q, R, etc.). These symbols will represent statements (i.e., sentences, propositions). The second kind of symbol we will use are logical operators that represent the relationship between statements. These connectives include "and," "or," "not," "if-then," and "if and only if" (represented by the symbols &, v, –,→, and ↔). Using these symbols allows us to clearly focus on the logical relationships between statements. In what follows, we will use formal logic to study deduction, which describes the necessary relationships between statements. As you will see below, in a deductive system there is no such thing as "probably." Either a statement is true or it is false. Further, and more importantly, certain true statements necessarily entail other statements. These features make deductive logic an incredibly powerful tool, even if in practice we must frequently rely on other forms of reasoning as well.

The system you are about to learn is a version of **statement logic** (also frequently called "propositional logic" or "sentential logic"). It is called statement logic because its primary unit of analysis is the statement (or proposition or sentence). If you go on to learn other kinds of formal logic you will realize that this is not the only possible formal system. There are higher-order logical systems, logical systems with different basic rules, and logical systems that do not take statements as their primary unit of analysis. Another important dimension of logic that is not detailed in this book is often called "informal logic" or "critical thinking." Informal logic attempts to provide an analysis of our everyday patterns of reasoning and provide tools for assessing under what conditions that reasoning is conducted well. Informal logic tends to use fewer symbols than formal logic, and it often avoids using some of the tools of formal logic such as truth tables or proofs. Formal and informal logic can be viewed as two approaches to the study of correct reasoning that exist at opposite ends of a spectrum. As one moves from one end of the spectrum to the other, they will find that the line between formal and informal logic can become blurred.

The version of logic you will learn in this text is one that approximates some forms of our everyday reasoning. Although the rules and operators you will learn may seem arcane by everyday standards, with a little imagination you will quickly see that this system can help clarify our own patterns of thought. This text aims to present a system of formal logic that can be fruitfully applied to real-world issues and help sharpen our everyday reasoning. This system should be seen as complementing, rather than competing with, presentations of informal logic. The student of good reasoning will be served well by studying both formal and informal approaches to logic.

I have endeavoured to present the information in an order that will make it most easily comprehendible. Later sections build on the skills developed in earlier sections. Being able to successfully answer the practice questions in each section should be a good indicator that you have grasped the important skills each section attempts to develop.

Karl Laderoute
University of Lethbridge

Preface for the Instructor

In my critical thinking course, I assign a text focused exclusively on informal logic. However, in that course students are required to learn the basics of statement logic, and I've been unable to find a suitably short book that can serve as a supplement for this purpose. My hope is that this text fills that need in a useful and affordable fashion.

This text is designed with three goals in mind. The first goal is approachability. Many students who are exposed to formal logic in their first or second year at university or college have no background in formal systems. In my view, some texts that explain such systems err by presupposing too much of their reader; my aim in this text is to explain statement logic without presupposing any knowledge of formal systems on the part of the student and to show the practical application of such systems.

The second goal of this text is affordability. Education is expensive enough in most places that students need not be exploited by obscene textbook costs. While in an ideal world, textbooks would all be free, I am very pleased that Broadview shares my vision that excellent texts need not be overly expensive for students.

The third goal is modularity. This text has been designed for easy use by the instructor. The first four chapters should be used to introduce students to the basic tools of formal logic. Then, depending on instructor preference and class time available, the remaining chapters can be covered in piecemeal fashion. Chapter 5 introduces students to the long truth table method and chapter 6 introduces them to the short truth table method. Chapter 6 should not be used without first covering chapter 5, but students need not learn the short truth table method to understand how formal logic operates. In my experience the short truth table method requires more class time to be effectively taught to students, so instructors pressed for time may wish to skip that method entirely in a course with learning aims other than a comprehensive introduction to statement logic. Chapters 7 through 9 cover natural deduction. Chapter 7 acts as a bridging chapter between truth tables and proofs. Truth tables are used to demonstrate why certain common argument forms are valid or invalid, and the valid common argument forms provide a basis for understanding the basic rules of inference introduced in chapter 8. Chapter 9 concerns advanced proof techniques, i.e., conditional proof and indirect proof. Chapter 10 examines replacement rules.

I have found that students respond well to learning the long truth table method in conjunction with the rules of inference: once students have a good grasp of how truth tables operate, it becomes easy to understand how and why the rules work as they do. However, instructors may opt to ignore truth tables entirely to focus on proof techniques instead. Depending on instructor interest and class time available, students may be exposed to only chapter 8 to gain an idea of how proofs operate, and they may be exposed to chapters 9 and 10 if time allows.

Ultimately this text aims to provide a flexible approach to teaching students statement logic in a way adaptable to the instructor's aims and available time. My sincere hope is that you and your students find this book to be a useful tool in your classroom.

Karl Laderoute
University of Lethbridge

Acknowledgments

I owe a great deal of thanks to many people who helped support the writing and publishing of this book in one way or another. I thank Stephen Latta at Broadview Press for seeing value in this project, encouraging me to see it through, and being very understanding with the delays the project saw between conception and completion. I also thank Bob Martin at Broadview Press for meticulously working through the draft material and suggesting numerous helpful changes. The final version of this text is much stronger thanks to Bob's insightful suggestions.

The Department of Philosophy at the University of Lethbridge was a welcoming intellectual home during the writing of this book. Thank you to each of the following members of that department for their encouragement and support of various pursuits: Kent Peacock, Bryson Brown, Michael Stingl, Katharina Stevens, Ardis Anderson, Victor Rodych, Paul Viminitz, and Gillman Payette. Particular thanks go to Katharina Stevens for providing feedback on an early draft of this project, and to Victor Rodych for several very long and very helpful email exchanges that helped clarify my thinking and show me what was important to achieve in this text. Thank you also to Jason Schultchen who proofread much of this book and provided helpful comments while a graduate student in the Department of Philosophy in Lethbridge. Neta Zaslow also read portions of this text and made fruitful suggestions for which I am grateful. Any mistakes remaining in the text are my own.

Thank you to my wife Ruthann for her love, support, encouragement, patience, and meticulous proof-reading! Thank you to my parents, Carrol and Joan, for their love and encouragement. Thank you to my parents-in-law, Michael and Andrea, for their love and support over the years. Lastly, thank you to Yoda for being there at the start of this project, and to Morbo for being there at its end.

Translating into Statement Logic

Symbolization

Most of us speak and think in a **natural language**, such as everyday English, French, or German. These languages have developed "naturally" over the course of human history. By contrast, formal logic is conducted in a **formal (or artificial) language,** much like mathematics. Artificial languages are created and developed with specific purposes in mind. Statement logic is intended to help us track truth relations between complex sets of statements and to make clear the patterns of reasoning that arguments utilize. In order to use formal logic, we must **translate** statements from a natural language into **symbolic form**. We will refer to this activity as **symbolization** when it is combined with representing the relationships between statements with **logical operators.**

In this chapter you will learn the basic rules for translating statements from natural language into symbolic form. You will also learn about the differences between simple and complex statements, and between inductive and deductive arguments. In chapters 2 through 4 we will continue examining how statements in natural language can be represented formally by letters and symbols. In chapter 2 we will explain how to construct and read basic truth tables. Chapter 3 will use truth tables to define logical operators which act as the "nuts and bolts" of formal logic. Along with defining those logical operators we will explain how truth tables can contain complex statements. Chapter 4 will explain how operators can be used to properly express statements and arguments in formal logic. In chapter 5 we see how truth tables can be used to test whether properly formulated deductive arguments are valid or invalid. Chapter 6 provides a short version of the truth table method for proving validity or invalidity. Chapters 7 through 10 provide an alternative way of testing arguments for (in)validity by way of using proofs. Ultimately truth tables and proofs are used to test deductive arguments for formal validity, and being able to do that allows us to distinguish a good deductive argument from a poor one.

1.1 Statements, Arguments, and Deduction

Sentences in a natural language (such as English) are often quite complex and there are many ways to convey the same basic thought with different sentences. Typically, we don't enjoy hearing or reading the exact same sequences of words over and over, and instead prefer some variety in what we hear and say. Statement logic is not concerned with being particularly enjoyable, which isn't to say that logic is inherently *unen-joyable*! Our main concern when we do logic is distinguishing truth from falsity. As a result, when we translate statements from natural language into symbolic form, we are primarily interested in creating the clearest possible version of what was expressed to assist us in distinguishing the true from the false. Our aim in symbolization is to analyze a given set of statements, separate out its basic units, assign a symbol to represent each of those units, and represent the relations between those units with other symbols.

A **statement** is any claim capable of being true or false. Some sentences are commands or questions, such as "shut the door" or "is today Tuesday?" Those kinds of sentences are not capable of being true or false. An **argument**, in the logical and philosophical sense, is a series of connected statements designed to provide reason for accepting another statement as true. One or more statements in an argument serve as **premises** while one or more other statements serve as **conclusions**. The simplest argument is a single premise that provides reason to believe a single conclusion. Many, if not most, arguments utilize more than one premise.

In this text we will regard "reasoning" to be the process of creating and evaluating arguments. There are two basic kinds of arguments, and hence two basic kinds of reasoning. This book is dedicated to the study of **deductive arguments**. The key feature of a valid deductive argument is that *the truth of the conclusion is guaranteed by the truth of the premises*. This feature makes deductive arguments very powerful. All deductive arguments are either formally valid or invalid. Only formally valid deductive arguments have the feature of the truth of the premises guaranteeing the truth of the conclusion. The techniques offered in this book for evaluating deductive arguments allow us to determine if any given deductive argument is formally valid or not. We will discuss formal validity in more depth in chapter 5.

The other basic kind of argument is the **inductive argument**. In an inductive argument, *the truth of the conclusion is not guaranteed by the truth of the premises*, although the truth of the premises in a good inductive argument will give some reason to believe the conclusion. Some inductive arguments will provide us with overwhelming reason to believe their conclusions while others will provide very scant evidence. We may refer to the evaluation of deductive arguments as deductive reasoning and the evaluation of inductive arguments as inductive reasoning. We may also refer to these processes as deduction and induction, respectively.

Learning about inductive arguments and how to evaluate them is important in developing your reasoning skills. Although this is a text in deduction, do not be intoxicated by the apparent certainty that deduction provides: deduction merely tells us what conclusions are entailed by (i.e., necessarily follow from) certain premises, but it does *not* tell us whether or not those premises are true. Humans are fallible creatures. When determining whether or not a given statement is true, we will almost inevitably rely on inductive reasoning to some extent. Induction and deduction should not be seen as rival forms of reasoning. Instead, they should be regarded as complementary.

1.2 Simple Statements, Complex Statements, and Truth Values

When translating statements, we must distinguish between **simple statements** and **complex statements**. Recall that a statement is any claim capable of being true or false. A **simple statement** is a statement that is not combined with any other statements and is not modified by a logical operator. Simple statements are the basic bearers of truth and falsity in statement logic, and we generally regard a simple statement as true when it corresponds to the way the world actually is.

Complex statements are statements modified by **logical operators**. We will use five logical operators in this book: − & v → ↔. Those symbols represent "not," "and," "or," "if ... then," and "if and only if." These operators modify the conditions under which a statement is true or false. Logical operators will be explained in detail in chapter 3.

Complex statements frequently combine simple statements together. Whenever you see more than one simple statement connected together, you have a complex statement. Additionally, when a statement is negated (i.e., something is claimed to be false), you have a complex statement. Whether a complex statement is true or false depends on what operator, or set of operators, modifies or connects its constituent simple statement(s) and the truth values of that simple statement (or those simple statements). A statement's **truth value** is its property of being either true or false, and we will regard every statement as actually having one of these two values (i.e., being true or false), even if we are unsure which value it has.

Many sentences in a natural language will contain more than one simple statement. The best way to determine what simple statements a sentence in natural language contains is to ask yourself this question: **can any part of this sentence be true while any other part of it is false?** Consider asking and answering this question as a test for determining what kind of statement you are dealing with. If the answer is "yes," then you are dealing with a complex statement. If the answer is "no," then you have found a simple statement. For example:

"Jeff went to the grocery store and he saw Sarah there."

It might be true that Jeff went to the grocery store while it may be false that he saw Sarah there. Hence, this sentence is a complex statement, because it has parts that can be independently true or false.

Bringing our analysis to the next level, we may break up our example sentence into smaller pieces and repeat our test:

"Jeff went to the grocery store."
"Jeff saw Sarah at the grocery store."

Asking our test question again, we now find that we have two simple statements. If it is true that "Jeff went to the grocery store," then it is simply true; no part of that sentence may be false while the other parts are true. Think about that for a moment. Can you make one part of that sentence true while another part is false? No, you can't (even if you say you can!). This is because a simple statement is the basic **truth bearer** of statement logic, and of human thought and language more generally. To be a truth bearer means to be the kind of thing that can be true or false. The phrase "grocery store" on its own can be neither true nor false. Saying "went to the grocery store" also cannot be true or false. Following the basic rules of English, we need a subject ("Jeff") and a predicate ("went to the grocery store") to have a full sentence that may be true or false.

Did you notice that in the original version of the sentence, what turned out to be two simple statements were conjoined by the word "and?" When you see "and" in a sentence, you may be dealing with a complex statement, though this is not guaranteed. Here are some examples of simple and complex statements:

Simple statements
   "Abdul walked through the park."
   "Morbo (the dog) likes to play with toys."
   "It is often windy in Lethbridge."

Complex statements
   "Abdul walked through the park and listened to Beethoven's ninth symphony."
   "Morbo (the dog) likes to play with toys and explore the garden."
   "If it is often windy in Lethbridge, then it will often be sunny there."

1.3 Symbolizing Arguments

Now that we are able to differentiate simple statements from complex statements, we can symbolize them. When symbolizing an argument, follow these steps:

1. **Determine how many simple statements are in the argument.**
2. **Clearly write out each simple statement.** Leave some space between them. Preferably, write each simple statement on a different line.
    i. Make simple statements affirmative. If you encounter a statement claiming something is false, treat it as a complex statement, and write out an affirmative version of the statement as your simple statement. E.g., "The weather is not nice today" is a complex statement. It is a negation of the simple statement "The weather is nice today."
    ii. Avoid pronouns whenever possible. Use proper nouns whenever possible, even if that requires restating what was originally said or written. The use of pronouns can lead to ambiguity and confusion when analyzing a complicated argument, which is why their use is to be avoided whenever possible. So, in our Jeff-and-the-grocery store example above, we designated the second simple statement as "Jeff [not 'he'] saw Sarah at the grocery store [not 'there']."
    iii. Use the present tense when writing out simple statements, unless noting a difference in tense (past, present, future) is required for the argument to make sense. As with avoiding pronouns, this may require you to rephrase the original statements.[1]
3. **Assign each simple statement a letter.** Do not use the same letter more than once.
    i. Do not assign complex statements a letter. Complex statements are formed by joining simple statements with symbols representing logical operators.

---

1. For a more detailed treatment of pronouns and tense, see the online supplement to this volume.

ii. Traditionally, the letters begin with *P* and follow sequentially (*P, Q, R*, ...). However, we need not follow that formula. If it makes sense to assign a particular letter to a particular simple statement, such as if a particular letter makes it easier to remember what that statement says, feel free to do so.

Let's look at an example:

"When It snows, Fred is late for work. If Fred is late for work again, he will be fired. It's snowing, so Fred will be fired."

Take a moment to run our simple statement test. How many simple statements are there in the example? The correct answer is three, and those statements stand in a particular logical relationship to one another (something we will examine more thoroughly in later chapters). Here are those three simple statements rewritten clearly and assigned a letter:

P = "It is snowing."
Q = "Fred is late for work."
R = "Fred will be fired."

Note that we had to add some extra words to fully capture the meaning of the original sentences while reproducing the three simple statements that it contained. We also left out some words from the original formulation in our rewritten statements. Such changes are perfectly acceptable when symbolizing statements.

Let's look at a second example:

"Jeff and Phil both offered to buy my car. Jeff offered more money for it, but he is unreliable, so I accepted Phil's offer instead."

We could symbolize those statements like this:

P = "Jeff offered to buy my car."
Q = "Phil offered to buy my car."
R = "Jeff offered me more money for it."
S = "He is unreliable."
T = "I accepted Phil's offer."

Note that R and S are imprecise in this formulation. We may ask what the "it" is in R and who "he" is in S. Also notice that R includes a comparison, though it does not currently include the full information needed to fully understand what the comparison is between. Let us rewrite our simple statements to be clearer:

P = "Jeff offered to buy my car."
Q = "Phil offered to buy my car."
R = "Jeff offered me more money than Phil for my car."
S = "Jeff is unreliable."
T = "I accepted Phil's offer for my car."

These rewritten versions of the simple statements are much clearer than before and less likely to cause confusion when analyzing an argument involving them. In general, try to be as precise as possible, omit irrelevant information, and be as clear as you can with the information that is included in your translations.

In some cases, there may be information that we don't need to capture in our symbolization because it's irrelevant to the actual argument we wish to evaluate. To know which information is and is not relevant we will need a better sense of how deductive arguments function. We will develop that sense over the coming chapters. Once we understand the various logical operators, their truth conditions, and argument forms, it will be much easier to judge what is and is not relevant when translating natural language sentences into simple statements. In some cases, even our relatively straightforward test for differentiating simple statements from complex statements can leave us wondering how our simple statements should read. The capacity for vagueness and ambiguity is a feature of natural language. Formal logic is a useful tool because it can help clarify our thinking, encouraging us to be more precise in our use of language in everyday contexts as well as our reasoning based on that natural language. In some cases, you may need to translate sentences in more than one way and then see which of those interpretations end up being most charitable based on your evaluation of the argument.

1.4 Practice Questions

Symbolize the following statements. Determine how many simple statements are in each example, rewrite the simple statements clearly (without pronouns), and assign each simple statement a letter. Answers to these questions are available in the online supplement for this text.

1. "Fred changed the oil in my car yesterday."
2. "Fred changed the oil in my car yesterday for free. He is such a nice guy."
3. "Formal logic is so dull and pointless!"
4. "Samantha really likes the original *Total Recall*, but she hates the remake."
5. "I don't feel so well today. I was around Jack yesterday, and he was ill, so I must have picked up whatever he had."
6. "Jennifer went to Italy last summer. While she was there, she saw the Colosseum and the Vatican. She also ate a lot of pasta."
7. "The fear of flying is completely irrational. You are far more likely to die on the way to the airport than while on the flight itself."
8. "My cat Whiskers is so nice to everyone…although he does kill birds."
9. "I will have salad instead of tacos for dinner."
10. "May I have gluten-free crust for my pizza?"

Truth Tables

This chapter will introduce **truth tables**. Understanding how to construct and read truth tables is fundamental to understanding formal logic. **Truth tables** are tables of truth values. The truth or falsity of a statement is referred to as its **truth value**. Truth tables use a series of columns and rows[2] to represent all possible combinations of true and false that the statements in an argument may have. Truth tables provide a guaranteed way for determining whether a given deductive argument is **formally valid** or **formally invalid**. When a deductive argument is formally valid, it is impossible for the argument's premises to be true when its conclusion is false. A good deductive argument must be valid.

To see formal validity or invalidity on a truth table, we must know how to read it. In section 2.1 we will learn how to read a truth table. Section 2.2 will provide rules for creating truth tables to represent statements and the arguments that statements make up. Section 2.3 will provide some examples to show how we create and read truth tables.

2.1 How to Read Truth Tables

Ultimately, we want to use truth tables to analyze arguments. Arguments are made up of statements. Truth tables allow us to examine

---

2. Having trouble remembering which one is vertical and which horizontal? Think of the columns in front of a Greek temple, or the columns in a newspaper, both of which are vertical.

every possible combination of true and false which the statements that make up an argument may have.

Let's return to an example presented in chapter 1 and modify it a little to make it an argument: "Morbo likes to play with toys. Morbo likes to explore the garden. So, Morbo likes to play with toys and explore the garden." This is a very simple argument that asserts that if both statements are true on their own, then they are true when asserted together. We can translate the simple statements like so:

P = "Morbo likes to play with toys."
Q = "Morbo likes to explore the garden."

Later we will learn much more about logical operators (symbols other than letters used in representing statements and arguments in formal logic). For now, we will introduce the simple operator "&." We use "&" to represent "and," just as we do in other contexts. The argument we have asserts that P is true, and Q is true, so P & Q is true (i.e., both statements are true). We can represent that on a truth table that looks like this:

Premise 1	*Premise 2*	*Conclusion*
P	Q	P & Q
T	T	T
T	F	F
F	T	F
F	F	F

Rows on a table run horizontally while columns run vertically. A "cell" is one box located at a particular place in a column and row. This table has five rows, three columns, and fifteen cells. As you will find out below, truth tables can have (almost) any number of columns, but the rows on these tables can only exist in fixed finite quantities.

The very first (top) row of a truth table simply identifies the parts of the argument it represents. We call this the "header row." Every truth table will contain a header row. We make a separate column for each simple statement (in this case P and Q) as well as for each complex statement: "P & Q" is a complex statement on this table. (Complex statements combine one or more statements with a logical operator. We will examine how these operators work in the next chapter.) We also label each premise and the conclusion of the argument so that we can easily identify them in the table.

It is also worth noting that not every column on a truth table will necessarily represent a premise or conclusion in an argument; some columns will represent individual statements involved in the argument but that are not a premise or conclusion. In our example above, each column does represent a premise or conclusion. More detailed comments on this point will be offered later.

Every row below the header row contains Ts and Fs. "T" stands for "True" and "F" stands for "False." In classical logic (what we are learning here), statements are either true or false; there are no other possibilities. We might not know the truth value of a given statement in an argument. That is fine! A truth table explores all of the possible combinations of truth and falsity for a given argument to determine its validity or invalidity. The exhaustive nature of formal logic in determining these possibilities is one of its great strengths.

Each column represents the possible truth values of a given statement in an argument. Each row is read across as a particular combination of truth values that is possible in the argument. For example, the first row on the example truth table above (the first row after the header row) represents a situation where all of the statements are true. The last row represents a situation where all of the statements are false. The other two rows represent situations where different combinations of statements are true and false.

Collectively, the rows on the table represent instances of every possible combination of the truth values of the simple statements for the argument we are examining. At any given time, only one row of truth values will correspond to reality (i.e., accurately represent the state of the world), but the table will contain every logically possible combination of those truth values. For instance, the second row of the table represents a possible situation where it is true that "Morbo likes to play with toys," it is false that "Morbo likes to explore the garden," and it is false that "Morbo likes to play with toys and explore the garden."

2.2 Basic Rules of Truth Table Formation

Although truth tables may seem complex, creating them is relatively simple. To create a truth table for any given argument, follow these steps:

1. **Identify all of the statements in the argument.**
   If the argument is provided in natural language, you will need to symbolize the argument at this point, as described in chapter 1.
2. **Create a header row. Starting at the left, create a column for each simple statement in the argument.**
   Remember, each simple statement will be represented by a different letter, so you should have one column for each letter in your argument.
3. **Add columns for each complex statement in the argument.**
   Remember, a complex statement is any statement that contains a logical operator or more than one simple statement. It is easy to differentiate between simple and complex statements after you have translated an argument because each simple statement will be represented by a single letter and complex statements will always include a logical operator (i.e., a symbol that is not a single letter). The symbolic representation of complex statements will be examined in-depth in chapter 3. If you have a complex statement with other complex statements within it, ensure you create a column for each complex statement on its own and when combined with other complex statements (more on this later).
4. **Label each premise and conclusion at the top of your truth table.**
5. **Determine the number of rows your table will require.**
   Your truth table will require 2^n **rows** *in addition* to the header row where n equals the number of simple statements in the

argument. For example, a truth table with 3 simple statements requires 2^3 rows (i.e., 8 rows) in addition to the header row; a truth table with 4 simple statements requires 2^4 rows (i.e., 16 rows) in addition to the header row.

6. **Enter the truth values in the cells in each column that represents a simple statement.**

In the left-most column under a simple statement, fill in the first half of your cells with T and the other half with F. Move to the next column (to the right), halve the number of Ts and Fs you insert at a time, and fill in the column. For every column to the right you move, halve the number of Ts and Fs you enter each time, but fill each column, so that the end result is always that each column is full of Ts and Fs, with the last column that represents a simple statement alternating between Ts and Fs in its cells. Continue this process until you have filled all of the cells in the columns of the simple statements only, leaving the cells in the columns representing complex statements empty for now.

For example: if your first column contains four Ts and four Fs, your second column will contain two Ts followed by two Fs followed by two more Ts and two more Fs. The third column would then alternate between Ts and Fs in the cells.

Filling in the simple statement columns is a mechanical process: there will never be variation in the pattern of Ts and Fs that fill the cells of these rows. Just remember to halve the number of Ts and Fs you add at a time as you move over each row. Your left-most column will always be half full of Ts and half full of Fs, with no alternating between them. The cells in the final simple statement column will always alternate between Ts and Fs.

7. **Enter the truth values in the cells in each column that represents a complex statement.**

Once we have filled in the truth values of all the simple statements on a truth table, we can then fill in the truth values for the complex statements on it as well. This process will be explained in chapter 3.

2.3 Example Truth Tables

Let's create some truth tables as examples. To do so, we will need example arguments. When we **write an argument** that we wish to test for validity, we number each step in the argument. In the final step we use the "∴" symbol to represent "therefore," signalling the conclusion of the argument. Here is a simple example argument in symbolic form written in this format:

1. P
2. ∴ Q

For our first example, let's use this argument: "Matt is playing video games. Therefore, Matt is happy." Now we will follow the steps provided in the previous section to create a truth table to represent this argument.

1. Identify all of the simple statements in the argument.
Now that we have an argument, our **first step** is to determine the number of simple statements it contains. If you begin with an argument in natural language, you will need to determine how many simple statements it contains when you symbolize the argument. If you begin with an already symbolized argument, then you simply need to determine how many different letters are used in the argument. There are two simple statements in our example argument, and we can represent those with the letters P and Q:

P = "Matt is playing video games."
Q = "Matt is happy."

2. Create a header row. Starting at the left, create a column for each simple statement in the argument.
Step two is to create a header row with those simple statements. Our header row will initially look like this:

P	Q

3. Add columns for each complex statement in the argument.
Our **third step** is to determine how many complex statements there are in our argument and add an extra column to our header row for each complex statement. In our example argument we have no complex statements, so we will not need to add any extra columns to our table.

4. Label each premise and conclusion at the top of your truth table.
Step four is to label the premises and conclusion in the argument. Remember that not every cell in the header row will necessarily be marked as a premise or conclusion, but every premise and conclusion in the argument will need to be marked above a cell in the header row. In our example we have one premise and a conclusion:

Premise 1	*Conclusion*
P	Q

5. Determine the number of rows your table will require.
Step five adds the additional[3] rows to the truth table. We need 2^n rows, where n equals the number of simple statements. Our table has two simple statements (P and Q), so we need $2^2 = 4$ rows. Let's add those rows now:

Premise 1	*Conclusion*
P	Q

---

3. Tip: there will always be an even number of rows in a truth table. The number of possible rows follows this progression: 2, 4, 8, 16, 32, 64, 128, 256, etc.

6. Enter the truth values in the cells in each column that represents a simple statement.

Now that we have the basic structure of our truth table, we need to fill in the truth values of each simple statement column following **step six** above. In our first column (the one that represents the statement P) we begin by filling in the first half of the rows with Ts and the second half of the rows with Fs:

Premise 1	Conclusion
P	Q
T	
T	
F	
F	

Once that is complete, we move to the next column to the right, in this case the column representing the statement Q. We halve the number of Ts and Fs entered at a time and fill the column (now entering one T followed by one F and repeating that process until the column is full):

Premise 1	Conclusion
P	Q
T	T
T	F
F	T
F	F

If our truth table contained any columns representing complex statements, we would now fill in the truth values in that column as our seventh and last step. However, because our truth table only contains simple statements, we are finished constructing this truth table. Once you have filled in *every* cell in a truth table you have completed constructing the truth table and can move on to testing the represented argument for validity. We will learn how to do that in chapter 5.

Before moving on, let's examine two more example truth tables in order of increasing complexity. For our next example, let's examine a truth table that represents this argument:

$$P$$

$$Q$$

$$\therefore R$$

Our **first step** is to determine the number of simple statements it contains. There are three simple statements in our example argument: P, Q, and R.

Step two is to create a header row with those simple statements. Our header row will initially look like this:

P	Q	R

Our **third step** is to determine how many complex statements there are in our argument and add an extra column to our header row for each complex statement. In our example argument we have no complex statements, so we will not need to add any extra columns to our table.

Step four is to label the premises and conclusion in the argument (remember that not every cell in the header row will necessarily be marked as a premise or conclusion, but every premise and conclusion in the argument will need to be marked above a cell in the header row):

Premise 1	Premise 2	Conclusion
P	Q	R

Step five adds the rows to the truth table. We need 2^n rows, where n equals the number of simple statements. Our table has three simple statements (P, Q, and R), so we need $2^3 = 8$ rows. Let's add those rows now:

Premise 1	Premise 2	Conclusion
P	Q	R

Now that we have the basic structure of our truth table, we need to fill in the truth values of each simple statement column following **step six** above. In our first column (the one that represents P) we begin by filling in the first half of the rows with Ts and the second half of the rows with Fs:

Premise 1	Premise 2	Conclusion
P	Q	R
T		
T		
T		
T		
F		
F		
F		
F		

Once that is complete, we move to the next column to the right (to the column representing Q). We halve the number of Ts and Fs entered at a time and fill the column (now entering two Ts followed by two Fs and repeating that process until the column is full):

Premise 1	Premise 2	Conclusion
P	**Q**	**R**
T	T	
T	T	
T	F	
T	F	
F	T	
F	T	
F	F	
F	F	

We still have one column that represents a simple statement (R), so we need to fill that in with Ts and Fs. Again, we halve the number of Ts and Fs we enter at a time, and fill the column. Because in the column representing Q, we entered two Ts followed by two Fs at a time, in this column we will alternate between adding a single T and a single F to fill the column:

Premise 1	Premise 2	Conclusion
P	**Q**	**R**
T	T	T
T	T	F
T	F	T
T	F	F
F	T	T
F	T	F
F	F	T
F	F	F

If our truth table contained any columns representing complex statements, we would now fill in the truth values in that column. However, because our truth table only contains simple statements, we are finished constructing this truth table.

Now let's construct an example truth table that contains complex statements. We will need to learn how to fill in those complex statements in the next chapter, but we can construct every part of the truth table except filling in the truth values for those complex statements based on what we already know. Here is the example argument we will use:

$$P \& Q$$
$$Q \to R$$
$$P \lor R$$
$$Q \leftrightarrow R$$
$$\therefore -R$$

Our **first step** is to determine the number of simple statements it contains. There are three simple statements in our example argument (P, Q, R). Remember, each simple statement is represented by a single letter, so no matter how complex the argument is, you simply need to count the number of different letters to determine how many simple statements are required on the table. Because we have the same number of simple statements in this example as we did in the previous example, many of the steps you took in constructing the previous table will be repeated here.

Step two is to create a header row with those simple statements. Our header row will initially look like this:

P	Q	R

Our **third step** is to determine how many complex statements there are in our argument and add an extra column to our header row for each complex statement. In our example argument we have five such statements: "P & Q," "Q → R," "P v R," "Q ↔ R," and "−R." We know that those are complex statements because they contain logical operators (& → v ↔ −), which we will examine in the next chapter. Most of those statements also contain more than one letter, which is another indicator that the statement is complex. Let's add those additional entries into our header row:

P	Q	R	P & Q	Q→R	P v R	Q↔R	–R

Step four is to label the premises and conclusion in the argument (remember that not every cell in the header row will necessarily be marked as a premise or conclusion, but every premise and conclusion in the argument will need to be marked above its cell in the header row):

			Premise 1	*Premise 2*	*Premise 3*	*Premise 4*	*Conclusion*
P	Q	R	P & Q	Q→R	P v R	Q↔R	–R

Step five adds the rows to the truth table. We need 2^n rows, where n equals the number of simple statements. Our table has three simple statements (P, Q, and R), so we need $2^3 = 8$ rows. Let's add those rows now:

			Premise 1	*Premise 2*	*Premise 3*	*Premise 4*	*Conclusion*
P	Q	R	P & Q	Q→R	P v R	Q↔R	–R

Now that we have the basic structure of our truth table, in **step six** we fill in the truth values of each simple statement column. The next table shows this all done:

			Premise 1	Premise 2	Premise 3	Premise 4	Conclusion
P	Q	R	P & Q	Q→R	P v R	Q↔R	−R
T	T	T					
T	T	F					
T	F	T					
T	F	F					
F	T	T					
F	T	F					
F	F	T					
F	F	F					

What we now have is a table that shows us all of the possible combinations of truth values for P, Q, and R. In the first row all three statements are true. In the last row they are all false. Every row in between the first and last row details a different possible combination of truth values. Together, our rows detail every possible combination of truth values that the simple statements may have.

At this point we turn to **step seven**, filling in the truth values for our complex statements. However, to do that, we need to understand how complex (i.e., truth functional) statements work, which we will turn to in the next chapter.

2.4 Practice Questions

1. What do truth tables try to determine or show (i.e., what is the point of creating a truth table)?
2. What is a "truth value"? What possible truth values may statements have?
3. What are the seven steps of truth table formation?
4. Is it possible for a truth table to have an odd number of rows, excluding the header row? Why or why not?
5. Is it possible for a truth table to have an odd number of columns? Why or why not?

Logical Operators

Logical operators (also frequently called "logical connectives") are the nuts and bolts of classical logic. Statements on their own do not form arguments in statement logic. Instead, arguments contain combinations of statements and logical operators (hereafter simply called "operators"). Simple statements are connected by operators, resulting in complex statements. There are five basic operators: negation, conjunction, disjunction, implication, and biconditional. In this chapter, we will learn how each of these operators work, as well as how to represent them on truth tables. In doing so, we will learn the seventh step of truth table formation, filling in the truth values for complex statements.

Before turning to the operators themselves, let's introduce a few concepts that will help us understand these operators. We will refer to what an operator connects as a **logical unit**. In their most basic function, operators modify or connect simple statements together to create complex statements. However, the operators can modify or connect complex statements to each other, creating increasingly complex statements. So, logical units may be either simple statements or complex statements. We will see how the use of brackets can help us connect very complex statements together in the next chapter.

All operators function with respect to a specific number of logical units. Negation is a **unary** (i.e., one-place) operator while conjunction, disjunction, implication, and the biconditional are all **binary** (two-place) operators. What this means is that negation operates on a single logical unit while conjunction, disjunction, implication, and the biconditional all connect (and hence operate on) two logical units. While P and Q will be used for example purposes in the following sections, any logical unit may be substituted in their place, i.e., the operators function the same way no matter what statements they operate on.

3.1 Negation

- Canonical English expression: "not"
- Represented with the symbol "−"

Negation is an operator that we find in common language all the time. **A negation tells us that the negated statement is false.** Negation is a unary operator because it operates on a single logical unit. A negation tells us that the logical unit that directly follows it is false. We will use "−" to represent negation in the rest of this book.[4]

Let's use an example featuring my dog whose name is Yoda. Yoda does *not* like to get wet. We can easily represent this fact using negation. Let the simple statement P be "Yoda likes to get wet." If we negate P, we are asserting that P is false. In natural language we can express negation in many ways, such as "it is false that Yoda likes to get wet" or "Yoda does not like to get wet." Negation is very simple yet incredibly important in statement logic. We can represent negation with a very simple truth table:

Negation Truth Table

P	−P
T	F
F	T

---

4. Note: the symbols that represent the operators are essentially arbitrary. Different logical systems may use different symbols to represent the exact same operation. For some other commonly used symbols, see the web supplement.

As you see on the table, –P is simply the opposite of P. When P is true, –P is false; when –P is true, P is false. Using our example above, let P mean "Yoda likes to get wet." When P is true, then it is true that "Yoda likes to get wet." If P is false, then –P is true: it is false that Yoda likes to get wet (i.e., Yoda does not like to get wet). –P is the negation of P, so if P means "Yoda likes to get wet," then –P will mean "Yoda does not like to get wet." When –P is true, then it is true that "Yoda does not like to get wet." When –P is false, then it is false that "Yoda does not like to get wet" (i.e., Yoda does like to get wet). This example shows us that a statement that is false is equivalent to the same statement's negation being true and vice versa.

The Negation Truth Table shows us how the truth value of –P depends on the truth value of P.

As a rule, make your symbolized simple statements affirmative in nature and negate them to show when something is false. For instance, "Ashley did not watch the new *Star Wars*" should be symbolized as: A = "Ashley watched the new *Star Wars*" which should then be negated as "–A".

3.2 Conjunction

- **Canonical English expression: "and"**
- **Represented with the symbol "&"**

Conjunctions combine two logical units together. This makes conjunction a binary operator. The logical units connected by a conjunction are called **conjuncts**. Conjunctions are most frequently noted by the word "**and**" in English. For example, the sentence "Karl and Yoda went for a walk and smelled beautiful flowers" contains a conjunction. There are two simple statements—"Karl and Yoda went for a walk" and "Karl and Yoda smelled beautiful flowers"—that are conjoined with the word "and." (Note that "Karl and Yoda" is not a conjunction in this sense. See below for some elaboration.) When we conjoin statements in this way, we are asserting that both statements are true. We will write the conjunction operator symbolically as "&". We can symbolize our sentence like so:

P = "Karl and Yoda went for a walk."
Q = "Karl and Yoda smelled beautiful flowers."
P & Q

"P & Q" reads "P is true and Q is true". **A conjunction simply asserts that both conjuncts are true.** We can represent the circumstances under which "P & Q" is true using a truth table.

Conjunction Truth Table

P	Q	P & Q
T	T	T
T	F	F
F	T	F
F	F	F

There is only one kind of possible situation when "P & Q" is true. "P & Q" is true only in the first row because that is the only row where both P and Q are true. In any instance where at least one of P or Q is false, their conjunction is false. The truth tables offered in this chapter are definitional, i.e., they define how the operators function based on the truth values of their constituent logical units. Once you know the conditions under which operators are true, you can determine their truth values on any given truth table that represents an argument.

Returning to a point made earlier, there is a special case where "and" is used in natural language worth noting. Is the following sentence a simple statement? "Karl and Yoda went for a walk." Having just mastered conjunctions, you may be tempted to symbolize that as two conjoined simple statements ("Karl went for a walk" and "Yoda went for a walk"). But that sentence probably doesn't mean that; it means that they went for a walk *together*. "Karl and Yoda went for a walk" may be restated as "Karl went for a walk with Yoda." Now the temptation to regard the statement as a conjunction rather than a simple statement is avoided. Understanding this kind of nuance is an important part of accurately symbolizing statements and in turn effectively using our formal system to evaluate arguments.[5]

3.3 Disjunction

- **Canonical English expression: "either ... or ..."**
- **Represented with the symbol "v"**

Disjunction is another common feature of spoken English and is canonically represented by the expression "either ... or ..." A disjunction is represented symbolically by the symbol "v". A disjunction connects two logical units (called **disjuncts**), which makes disjunction a binary operator. In statement logic, the disjunction operator **claims that** *at least one* **of the disjuncts is true.** The disjunction truth table will clarify:

Disjunction Truth Table

P	Q	P v Q
T	T	T
T	F	T
F	T	T
F	F	F

As you can see, the only time an inclusive disjunction is false is when both disjuncts are false. When at least one disjunct is true, the disjunction is true.

Disjunction works a little differently than it sometimes does in natural language. Often, in natural language, when we say, for example, "Either you can have peas *or* carrots," we mean that "either you can have peas, *or* carrots, *but not both peas and carrots.*" That kind of disjunction

---

5. For another way in which 'and' in English doesn't exactly match '&', see the web supplement.

is called an *exclusive disjunction*—that is, 'or' means one or another *but not both*. But in statement logic, when we represent "either ... or ..." with 'v' we mean "either this *or* that *or both this and that*." This kind of disjunction is called an **inclusive disjunction**.

We can illustrate the use of disjunction with another example: "either Yoda is taking a nap or Yoda is in the garden." In ordinary English we may be tempted to understand this statement as claiming that "either Yoda is taking a nap or Yoda is in the garden, *but not both*." However, the statement is here meant inclusively: "either Yoda is taking a nap or Yoda is in the garden, or *both* Yoda is taking a nap and she is in the garden" (i.e., Yoda is taking a nap in the garden).

Whether a statement in ordinary English is meant as an inclusive or exclusive disjunction is a contextual matter. In the example just given, it could be the case that Yoda never naps in the garden, under which circumstances the disjunction would have been meant exclusively. Sometimes it is very easy to tell if a disjunction is meant exclusively, such as when a contradiction or impossibility would result from both disjuncts being true. E.g., "either today is Tuesday or today is Thursday." If that statement were meant inclusively, then the speaker would be allowing for the possibility that the same day would be both Tuesday and Thursday, which is obviously impossible. As we will see in the next chapter, we can formulate an exclusive disjunction by combining multiple operators. We will simply call inclusive disjunctions "disjunctions" until section 4.2 where exclusive disjunctions are discussed in detail.

3.4 Implication

- Canonical English expression: "if ... then ..."
- Represented by the symbol "→"

Implication statements (often called "conditional statements") also represent a relationship between two logical units, and so implication is a binary operator. We often discuss implications when we discuss causal sequences or rules. For instance, "If you flip the switch, then the light will come on" and "If you cross-check, then you will get a penalty." Another use shows dependency of one fact on another: "If Sam goes to the party, Irma will too."

The two logical units joined by an implication statement are called the **antecedent** and the **consequent**. In the logical statement "P → Q", the antecedent is the first unit, the "if" part (P), while the consequent is the second unit, the "then" part (Q); and this means if P then Q. In natural language, the antecedent sometimes does not come first. In "Irma will go to the party if Sam goes" the "if" part comes second. It can be rephrased as "If Sam goes to the party, Irma will go too." So one symbolization stands for both: using the obvious letters, S → I. The order of statements in natural language does not dictate which logical unit acts as the antecedent and which acts as the consequent; it is their *logical* relationship that matters, and that is determined by the relationship between the units' truth values.

The truth table for the implication statement is a little trickier than the other truth tables we have examined:

Implication Truth Table

P	Q	P → Q
T	T	T
T	F	F
F	T	T
F	F	T

Notice that there is only one situation where the implication statement is false: **an implication statement is false when (and *only* when) the antecedent is true and the consequent is false.** An implication statement operates this way because it claims that "if the antecedent is true, then the consequent must be true as well." For instance, if Sam goes to the party but Irma doesn't, then that implication statement above is false.

It is important to note that the truth value of an implication statement is completely determined by the truth values of the antecedent and the consequent. This means that implication statements often do not perfectly correspond to our intuitive understanding of when such statements are true. For instance, rows three and four on the table may seem puzzling. You may be asking: why is the implication statement true whenever the antecedent is false? Because implication statements read "if the antecedent is true, then the consequent must be true as well," such statements say nothing about cases where the antecedent is false. For example, if Sam *doesn't* go to the party, Irma may or may not go: the implication statement doesn't commit to any outcome here. So is that implication statement true or false when neither goes, or when just Sam doesn't? This isn't clear in ordinary language; but logical statements must be true or false, so (for reasons we won't go into here) logicians prefer that an implication statement is taken to be true whenever its antecedent is false—or, for that matter, whenever its consequent is true.[6]

3.5 Biconditional

- Canonical English expression: "if and only if"
- Represented by the symbol "↔"

The biconditional is our last operator and is also a binary operator. We will represent the biconditional with a double-arrow (↔). A biconditional is usually expressed in English by "if and only if." A biconditional claims that either **both logical units are true or both are false**. For instance,

(P) Joe is a bachelor *if and only if* (Q) Joe is an unmarried male.

That means that

---

6. A more detailed explanation of the seemingly counterintuitive nature of implication statements is available in the online supplement to this book.

If (P) Joe is a bachelor, then (Q) he is an unmarried male,

and

If (Q) Joe is an unmarried male, then (P) he is a bachelor.

Either both simple statements are true or both are false.

Here is the definitional truth table for the biconditional:

Biconditional Truth Table

P	Q	P ↔ Q
T	T	T
T	F	F
F	T	F
F	F	T

We can see from this truth table that the biconditional is true only if both of the units on which it operates have the same truth value.

As we saw above, the implication statement does not always adequately capture what we mean when we make statements that include "if" in English. For example, Jon asks Tom if he is coming to the party. Tom replies "yes, if I get my work done before tonight." If Tom's statement is interpreted as an implication statement (P → Q), then Tom may or may not show up to the party if he does *not* get his work done before tonight; if the work is not done, then the antecedent of the implication statement is false, which means we have no information concerning whether or not the consequent will be true or false. But Tom obviously means that he *will* be at the party if his work is done and he *will not* be at the party if his work is not done (P ↔ Q). Interpreting Tom's "if" as an "*if and only if*" captures this meaning well.

3.6 Example Truth Table Revisited

Recall our example truth table in chapter 2. We can now fill in columns we had to leave blank. Here is the example again:

			Premise 1	*Premise 2*	*Premise 3*	*Premise 4*	*Conclusion*
P	Q	R	P & Q	Q→R	P v R	Q↔R	−R
T	T	T					
T	T	F					
T	F	T					
T	F	F					
F	T	T					
F	T	F					
F	F	T					
F	F	F					

We can fill in the fourth column by following the rules of conjunction. Read across each row to see if both P and Q are true, and fill in the truth values for each cell of the "P & Q" column accordingly. Remember, a conjunction is true only when both conjuncts are true. In any other circumstance, the conjunction is false. Our fourth column will look like this once we fill in each cell:

			Premise 1	Premise 2	Premise 3	Premise 4	Conclusion
P	Q	R	P & Q	Q → R	P v R	Q ↔ R	–R
T	T	T	T				
T	T	F	T				
T	F	T	F				
T	F	F	F				
F	T	T	F				
F	T	F	F				
F	F	T	F				
F	F	F	F				

Note that "P & Q" is true only in the first two rows, because those are the only two rows where both P and Q are true. Because R is not part of P & Q, the truth value of R is simply irrelevant to determining the truth value of P & Q.

We can fill in the remaining columns by following the same method of reading across each row to see the truth value of the logical units that make up the complex statement. The next column represents the complex statement Q → R. We can fill in each cell in that row by reading across the row to see the truth values of Q and R. Remember that an implication statement (like Q → R) is false only when the antecedent (Q in this case) is true and the consequent (R in this case) is false. We check each row. Where Q is true and R is false, we mark Q → R as false. In all other rows we mark Q → R as true:

		Conclusion	Premise 1	Premise 2			
P	Q	R	P & Q	Q → R	P v R	Q ↔ R	−R
T	T	T	T	T			
T	T	F	T	F			
T	F	T	F	T			
T	F	F	F	T			
F	T	T	F	T			
F	T	F	F	F			
F	F	T	F	T			
F	F	F	F	T			

The next column represents P v R. That complex statement is false only when both disjuncts (P and R in this case) are false. We read across each row to check the truth values of P and R, and then fill in the value of P v R based on those:

		Conclusion	Premise 1	Premise 2			
P	Q	R	P & Q	Q → R	P v R	Q ↔ R	−R
T	T	T	T	T	T		
T	T	F	T	F	T		
T	F	T	F	T	T		
T	F	F	F	T	T		
F	T	T	F	T	T		
F	T	F	F	F	F		
F	F	T	F	T	T		
F	F	F	F	T	F		

The next column represents Q ↔ R. A biconditional statement is true when both logical units connected by the operator are true or false. A biconditional statement is false when the truth values of the two logical units are not the same. In this case, Q ↔ R is true when Q and R are either both true or false. Q ↔ R is false when Q is true and R is false or vice versa. Let us fill in those values now:

			Conclusion	Premise 1	Premise 2		
P	Q	R	P & Q	Q → R	P ∨ R	Q ↔ R	−R
T	T	T	T	T	T	T	
T	T	F	T	F	T	F	
T	F	T	F	T	T	F	
T	F	F	F	T	T	T	
F	T	T	F	T	T	T	
F	T	F	F	F	F	F	
F	F	T	F	T	T	F	
F	F	F	F	T	F	T	

The final column represents −R. A negation is true whenever the negated logical unit is false. In this case, −R is true whenever R is false and vice versa. We will fill in the truth values for −R by reading across the row and inserting the correct truth value in each cell:

		Conclusion	Premise 1	Premise 2			
P	Q	R	P & Q	Q → R	P v R	Q ↔ R	–R
T	T	T	T	T	T	T	F
T	T	F	T	F	T	F	T
T	F	T	F	T	T	F	F
T	F	F	F	T	T	T	T
F	T	T	F	T	T	T	F
F	T	F	F	F	F	F	T
F	F	T	F	T	T	F	F
F	F	F	F	T	F	T	T

We have now finished this truth table! Remember that the truth tables presented in sections 3.1–3.5 are definitional, i.e., they define under what conditions each kind of complex statement is true or false. The truth table offered in this section provides an example of how each kind of complex statement's truth values can be determined on a truth table. If any of the steps taken in this section seem confusing, consider revisiting the discussion of the relevant operators in the sections above.

3.7 Practice Questions

1. Recreate the truth table for negation from memory.
2. Recreate the truth table for conjunction from memory.
3. Recreate the truth table for disjunction from memory.
4. Recreate the truth table for implication statements from memory.
5. Recreate the truth table for biconditional statements from memory.

Translate the following sentences into symbolic form. Add the appropriate logical operators to capture the logical relationship between statements where appropriate:

6. "Sam went to the park and saw Jeff there."
7. "Jessica and Susan went to the park together."
8. "If Phil didn't answer his door, then he must not be home."
9. "You can have cake or pie for dessert."
10. "A piece of furniture is a chair if and only if it is designed to be sat on."
11. "Where there's smoke, there's fire."
12. "Ahmed can ride the rollercoaster, go on the bumper cars, or do both one after the other."

CHAPTER 4

Brackets and Well-Formed Formulas

4.1 Brackets and Well-Formed Formulas
4.2 Exclusive Disjunction
4.3 Practice Questions

4.1 Brackets and Well-Formed Formulas

Here we will introduce the notion of a **well-formed formula (WFF for short)**. A WFF (frequently pronounced "woof" or "wiff") is simply a statement that is formulated according to the syntactical rules of our formal language. Just as statements in a natural language must follow certain (grammatical) rules of formulation, so too must the statements of formal logic. For instance, "Yoda went to the dog park ate her dinner" is not a well-formulated sentence in English because it contains two predicates and one subject. "Yoda went to the dog park and ate her dinner or took a nap" is also problematic because it is hard to determine exactly what is meant: is the assertion that Yoda went to the dog park and ate her dinner *or* she took a nap (rather than, or in addition to, eating her dinner and going to the park)? Or is the assertion that Yoda went to the dog park and additionally ate her dinner or took a nap (or both)? Those two formulations have different truth conditions when we think about the operators involved. Similarly, "P & Q v R" is not a well-formed formula in statement logic because it is not clear where the conjunction and disjunction are supposed to begin and end, or which logical units they are supposed to connect.

All simple statements are WFFs. Complex statements that connect the appropriate number of logical units are also WFFs. Always remember that **for a complex statement to be a WFF, each operator must be clearly attached to its corresponding number of logical units**. These rules govern the formation of WFFs:

1. **An operator must connect the appropriate number of logical units (one for negation, two for all other operators).**
    *   "P Q" is not allowed, but the following are allowed: "P & Q" "P v Q" "P → Q" "P ↔ Q"
    *   "P &" and "& Q" are not allowed because the conjunction only has one conjunct. "P & Q" is allowed because the conjunction connects two conjuncts. The same rules apply for the other three binary operators (disjunction, implication, and biconditional).
    *   "P −Q" is not allowed because negation is a unary operator, which means it only affects the Q, and we do not have any other operator to connect the P and −Q together. Because negation is a unary operator, any simple statement can be negated and form a WFF (e.g., "−P").

2. **Two binary operators cannot follow each other, but a negation may come directly *after* any operator, so long as it comes before a logical unit.**
    *   "P & v Q" is not allowed because two binary operators cannot follow each other. The following examples are also not allowed for the same reason: "P v & Q" "P → & Q" "P & → Q" "P v → Q" "P → v Q" "P ↔ & Q" "P ↔ → Q"
    *   "P & −Q" is allowed because the negation comes immediately *after* the binary operator (in this case a conjunction).
    *   "P − & Q" is not allowed because the negation comes immediately *before* a binary operator (in this case a conjunction).
    *   "− −P" is allowed because the second negation comes after another operator, which in this case happens to be another negation.

3. **Whatever is contained within brackets (parentheses) constitutes a logical unit, and when a binary operator comes directly before or after brackets then it takes whatever is contained within the brackets as one of the logical units it connects. Finally, brackets (parentheses) must always come in pairs.**

- Because negation is a unary operator, when modifying a logical unit in brackets it must come before that unit and effectively negates the unit as a whole by claiming that what is contained within the brackets is false.

- "(P & Q) & (R & S)" is a WFF. Each conjunction operates on two logical units because it is a binary operator. Inside each set of brackets is a WFF produced in accordance with the rules above. These units are then operated on by the conjunction between them.

- "−(P v Q)" is a WFF; what's negated is the whole logical unit inside the brackets.

- "P → (Q" is not a WFF because there is a single bracket. All brackets must come in pairs. Any complex statement with an odd number of brackets is not a WFF.

Here are some examples to help illustrate how these rules work. All of these are WFFs:

- P
- P & Q
- P & (Q & R)
- P v Q
- P → (−Q v R)
- − − − −P v (Q → R)

None of the following formulas are WFFs. See if you can explain why by looking at the rules we have already introduced:

- P − & Q
- P Q
- P → (Q

- P v & Q
- P → Q R
- P v (Q & R → S)

Now that we've introduced the rules governing WFFs, let's look more closely at how brackets function. Brackets and parentheses are used in statement logic as they are used in mathematics: to clarify how we are to read certain expressions. Brackets are sometimes called "square brackets," and parentheses "round brackets," respectively. They look like this: "[ ]" and "( )". For the sake of simplicity, we will simply call both of these "brackets" for now.

Whatever is contained within the brackets constitutes a logical unit, and multiple sets of brackets may be used to create complex units that contain multiple units within them (just like a single system can contain multiple subsystems each of which have their own parts). In the previous chapter we only connected simple statements with our logical operators. However, logical operators can operate on complex statements themselves, so long as the correct number of logical units are involved (one logical unit for negation, two logical units for the other operators).

Failing to use brackets often leads to uncertainty. Using our example above, our exact meaning is unclear if we write "P & Q v R". We now know that both conjunction and disjunction are binary operators, but we currently have three logical units in each complex statement where we should have only two in each. The result is a formula that is *not* well formed because each of those operators must connect two logical units.

Do P and Q belong together as a logical unit, meaning that the disjuncts are "R" and "P and Q"? Or does P stand by itself as a conjunct, with "Q or R" as the other conjunct? The use of brackets helps clarify the exact meaning of symbolized statements. These statements, however, are WFFs—they are unambiguous.

(P & Q) v R
P & (Q v R)

As noted above, these two complex statements have two different sets of truth conditions, and we can clearly represent the two cases using one truth table:

P	Q	R	P & Q	(P & Q) v R	Q v R	P & (Q v R)
T	T	T	T	T	T	T
T	T	F	T	T	T	T
T	F	T	F	T	T	T
T	F	F	F	F	F	F
F	T	T	F	T	T	F
F	T	F	F	F	T	F
F	F	T	F	T	T	F
F	F	F	F	F	F	F

As we can see here, (P & Q) forms a complex statement in which P and Q are conjuncts. That conjunction serves as a single logical unit embedded within a disjunction. In the complex statement "(P & Q) v R", the complex statement (P & Q) serves as a single disjunct while R serves as the other disjunct.[7]

When adding brackets to complex statements, we must be careful to ensure that we are adding pairs of brackets where required to make our formulas well-formed. For example, there is no logical difference between P and (P), or −P and (−P), or P & Q and (P & Q). But there is a logical difference between (P & Q) v R and P & (Q v R). Generally speaking, only add brackets where they are needed, and brackets are needed to identify which logical units are modified by an operator. When an operator comes directly before or after a set of brackets, everything contained within that set of brackets acts as one of the logical units that operator modifies.

In the rest of this book, round brackets (parentheses) will be used as the default notation to enclose statements. When more than one set

---

7. For a more thorough explanation of what the truth table shows us about these statements, refer to the online supplement to this book.

of brackets is required for the sake of clarity, round and square brackets will be used in an alternating fashion. E.g., P & (Q v [R → (S ↔ T)]).

One more note on the use of brackets: **a negation before a bracket negates the logical unit within the brackets**. −P simply means P is false. If we have (−P & Q), then we are stating that not-P is true (i.e., P is false) and Q is true. However, −(P & Q) means that P & Q is false, i.e., it is not true that both P and Q are true. To see how this placement of brackets makes a difference (and for practice at doing truth tables), draw a truth table whose header row contains one column for each of these statements: P, Q, −P, (−P & Q), (P & Q), −(P & Q). When you are done, compare your answer with the truth table below:

P	Q	−P	−P & Q	P & Q	−(P & Q)
T	T	F	F	T	F
T	F	F	F	F	T
F	T	T	T	F	T
F	F	T	F	F	T

Easy, right? Once you've mastered the basic use of brackets, the world of logic is your (metaphorical) oyster. We can embed complex statements within complex statements within complex statements. What a dream (or nightmare!).

Let's look at one last example of such a complex affair. Before we do that, here is one tip: add a column to your truth table for each complex statement contained in an argument. This includes adding a separate column for each logical unit, including each distinct complex statement within larger complex statements. As a general rule, increase the complexity of your statements as you move to the right of your table. The left-most columns should all be simple statements, and as the columns move towards the right, they should contain increasingly complex statements.

This tip is not an absolute rule because there is nothing technically incorrect about arranging information differently on a truth table. Sometimes you will also find it helpful to change the order of your columns to group together complex statements that relate to each other in the argument. With this tip in mind, let's look at the last example argument of this section:

1. P & (Q v [R → S])
2. R
3. R → S
4. ∴ Q

Here is the argument represented on a truth table:

Conclusion		Premise 2		Premise 3		Premise 1
P	Q	R	S	R → S	Q v (R → S)	P & (Q v [R → S])
T	T	T	T	T	T	T
T	T	T	F	F	T	T
T	T	F	T	T	T	T
T	T	F	F	T	T	T
T	F	T	T	T	T	T
T	F	T	F	F	F	F
T	F	F	T	T	T	T
T	F	F	F	T	T	T
F	T	T	T	T	T	F
F	T	T	F	F	T	F
F	T	F	T	T	T	F
F	T	F	F	T	T	F
F	F	T	T	T	T	F
F	F	T	F	F	F	F
F	F	F	T	T	T	F
F	F	F	F	T	T	F

Wow! Before reading the explanation of this truth table, take a few moments to see if you can figure out how it works.

If that truth table made perfect sense, then you are doing quite well. If you ran into some trouble, don't worry too much. This truth table is a bit harder to decipher than anything we've looked at previously. Let's examine its construction in detail:

First, we have four simple statements on our truth table, each represented by a different letter (P, Q, R, and S). Recalling our formula that we require 2^n rows on a truth table in addition to the header row tells us that we require 2^4 rows, which is 16 rows.

A complication in this truth table is that there is a column for an implication statement within a disjunction within a conjunction. But this is not difficult to handle. Notice how the statements in the header row build up that complex statement bit by bit, from left to right. As a rule, add whatever columns you need to keep track of the truth values of all of the components in your argument, including the various logical units of complex statements such as P & (Q v [R → S]). Also recall the tip above to order your columns so that their contents increase in complexity as you move to the right of your table. Lastly, don't forget to label your premises and conclusion. Although we need a lot of information to construct complex truth tables, when we assess arguments for validity and invalidity it is only the columns representing the premises and conclusion that we will need to utilize. We will discuss assessing arguments for validity and invalidity in the next chapter.

4.2 Exclusive Disjunction

In section 3.3 we discussed inclusive and exclusive disjunction. In natural language, we use "or" in different ways—sometimes we mean "inclusive or" (i.e., P or Q, or both P and Q), and other times we mean "exclusive or" (i.e., P or Q, but not both). The disjunction operator always represents "inclusive or." But we can also represent "exclusive or" in statement logic by using a combination of other operators and brackets. Remember from section 3.3 that the exclusive disjunction reads "this or that, and not both this and that." Can you think of how we might formulate such a complex statement using the five basic operators and brackets? The natural language formulation should provide some hints: we will need to use disjunction, conjunction, and negation.

Let us simply use P and Q to represent our simple statements "this" and "that" (which themselves might really be anything because those words are pronouns). We already know that we will require a disjunction which will look like this:

P v Q

Next, we need to represent the fact that we are not allowed to have both P and Q be true at the same time. Recall our discussion of negation in this chapter: when a bracketed unit is negated, we are simply asserting that the bracketed unit is false. So, we represent "not both this and that" as the negated conjunction of the two, because the negated conjunction asserts that they cannot both be true at the same time. The negated conjunction looks like this:

–(P & Q)

Now we need to combine these two complex statements into a single complex statement that uses each of these statements as a single logical unit. We will need to conjoin these two statements together, which will look like this:

(P v Q) & –(P & Q)

This symbolization now reads how we want it to read. Note that the negation applies to the entire conjunction in brackets. This whole complex statement is a WFF because the main conjunction combines two logical units, each of which are WFFs in their own right. The negation modifies the second logical unit of the main conjunction because it is outside of the brackets. Our symbolization claims that "either P is true or Q is true or both are true, *and* it is false that P and Q are both true." That leaves the remaining possible truth conditions as either P is true or Q is true but they cannot both be true at the same time. Let's see these truth conditions on a truth table:

| | *Inclusive* | | *Exclusive* | | |
P	Q	P v Q	P & Q	–(P & Q)	(P v Q) & –(P & Q)
T	T	T	T	F	F
T	F	T	F	T	T
F	T	T	F	T	T
F	F	F	F	T	F

As you can see, the exclusive disjunction is true only when either P or Q is true, but not when both P and Q are true, and that is precisely what we wanted to capture from our natural language formulation.

As mentioned earlier, one of the benefits of studying formal logic is becoming more precise with our natural language statements. The difference in the truth conditions between an inclusive and exclusive disjunction serves as an example of this kind of precision. The five basic operators of statement logic can be combined into various complex statements to capture complex relationships among truth values, which makes this formal system a powerful tool once mastered.

4.3 Practice Questions

Translate and symbolize the following statements, using brackets as required to accurately capture their meaning:

1. "If you buy a donut at Terry's Coffee Shop, they give you a muffin and a coffee for free!"
2. "You can advance the presentation by pressing spacebar or left-clicking on the mouse."
3. "Receiving one more piece of bad news today will be enough to make me lose my mind!"
4. "Ruthann is intelligent, funny, and very talented."
5. "You can have soup, salad, or fries. We have a special on, so you can have all three if you want."
6. "Priya will go to Jerome's party as long as she finishes her logic practice and it isn't raining."
7. "Applicants must possess a bachelor's degree to be qualified for the position."
8. "No shirt, no shoes, no service."
9. "Either it will be cloudy and raining tomorrow or the sun will shine, but not both."
10. "As long as Juan has free time on Saturday, hasn't twisted his ankle, and feels like doing it, he'll go for a walk in the coulees."

PART II

Testing Validity with Truth Tables

CHAPTER 5

The Long Truth Table Method

5.1 Validity and Soundness
5.2 The Long Truth Table Method for Testing Validity
5.3 Practice Questions

Now that we know how to translate natural language statements into symbolic form, connect those statements with operators, and create truth tables to represent the arguments they make up, we can use truth tables to test arguments for validity and invalidity. There are two truth table methods for testing the validity of deductive arguments, **the long truth table method** and **the short truth table method**. Ultimately both methods try to find a possible situation where the conclusion of an argument is false and all of its premises are true. If we can find such a situation (represented by a row on the table), then the argument is invalid. If we cannot find such a possibility, then the argument is valid.

You need to understand the long method in order to be able to use the short method, so we will begin by examining the long method in this chapter. Before doing that, we will discuss formal validity in more detail to clarify what truth tables can show us.

5.1 Validity and Soundness

When using formal logic we want to do more than merely symbolize statements. Ultimately, we want to evaluate arguments. Recall that an **argument** is a series of statements, some of which act as **premises** that offer reason, support, or justification for one or more other statements that act as **conclusions.** In deductive reasoning, a good argument is a **formally valid** argument with true premises.

Formal validity concerns the structure, not the content, of a deductive argument. As noted in chapter 1, when a deductive argument is formally valid, it has the following feature: **the premises, if true, guarantee the truth of the conclusion.** Stated differently, it cannot be the case that the conclusion of a formally valid argument is false if all of its premises are true.[8] Note that the converse does not hold! The conclusion of a formally valid argument may be true when one (or more) of its premises is false: in that case, the conclusion *happens* to be true, independently of the reasons provided in the argument. A deductive argument is **formally invalid** when it is not formally valid; all deductive arguments are either formally valid or formally invalid. Moving forward, we will typically shorten these terms to "valid" and "invalid."

Here are examples of *invalid* arguments:

- **Either it is raining or it is snowing. It is raining. So it is snowing.**
- **If a week contains eight days, then a year has twelve months. A week does not contain eight days. Therefore a year has twelve months.**
- **If pigeons are reptiles, then triangles have three sides. Triangles have three sides, so pigeons are reptiles.**

Those arguments are invalid because even if the premises are true, the truth of the premises does not guarantee the truth of the conclusion.

Here are examples of *valid* arguments:

- **Either Carrol is hunting or Carrol is fishing. Carrol is not fishing. Therefore, Carrol is hunting.**
- **If it is raining, then Joan has an umbrella. It is raining. So, Joan has an umbrella.**
- **If Morbo is chewing on sticks, then Morbo is happy. Morbo is not happy. Therefore, Morbo is not chewing on sticks.**

---

8. You will notice that formal validity is governed by the implication statement "If the premises of a formally valid argument are true then the conclusion of that argument must be true as well."

- If the author of this book is an alien, then Toronto is west of Calgary. Toronto is not west of Calgary. So, the author of this book is not an alien.
- If the Earth has two moons, then Vancouver is east of Winnipeg. The Earth has two moons. Therefore, Vancouver is east of Winnipeg.

These are all valid arguments because the truth of the premises in each argument guarantees the truth of the conclusion. The last example is bizarre because it is false that the Earth has two moons. Additionally, the number of moons orbiting Earth has no sensible connection to the physical location of Vancouver and Winnipeg. Despite those oddities, the last example contains a *valid* argument, although it is not a *sound* argument. Remember, an argument can be valid even if it has false premises.[9]

A deductive argument is **sound** when it is both formally valid and has true premises. In a sound argument the truth of the premises is "preserved" in the conclusion. We call valid arguments "truth preserving" because every inference in a valid argument preserves truth, such that if the premises are true then so must be the conclusion. Formally invalid deductive arguments are bad deductive arguments because they are not truth preserving, i.e., the truth of the premises is not necessarily preserved in the conclusion, which is the whole aim of deduction. Somewhat like plumbing, we want our deductive arguments to give us out one end what we put in the other (water for water, truth for truth).

Truth tables are used to test deductive arguments for validity or invalidity. Because truth tables examine every possible combination of truth values that the statements which make up an argument may have, they allow us to see if there are any possible situations where all of the premises of an argument are true while the conclusion is false. If such a situation exists, then the argument is invalid; if no such situation exists, then the argument is valid.

As discussed in the first chapter, determining whether or not premises are (likely) true or false is a very important part of arguing well. However, the tools of formal logic themselves usually do not help us with this part of arguing. Informal logic more directly concerns itself with determining whether or not premises are true (or likely true),

---

9. See the supplementary website for some odd facts about validity.

which is why formal and informal logic should both be seen as valuable tools for an independent reasoner.

5.2 The Long Truth Table Method for Testing Validity

Let's start with this example argument:

"**If it's Thursday, then it's not Tuesday. It's Thursday, so it must not be Tuesday.**"

It may seem intuitively obvious that this argument is valid. Let's see how the truth table method confirms that for us. First, we need to translate this argument. The result is this:

P = "It is Thursday."
Q = "It is Tuesday."

Next, we need to add our logical operators to provide a full symbolic representation of the argument. The result is this:

1. P → –Q
2. P
3. ∴ –Q

Now we can construct a truth table to fully explore the possible truth conditions of all of the variables:

Premise 2		Conclusion	Premise 1
P	Q	–Q	P → –Q
T	T	F	F
T	F	T	T
F	T	F	T
F	F	T	T

Note that we have labelled our premises and conclusion above the header row of the appropriate columns. This step is very important when we want to test for validity. Now that we have a full truth table mapping out our argument, we can test the argument for validity, which is really quite easy.

Recall that a deductive argument is valid when the truth of the premises guarantees the truth of the conclusion. This means that, in a valid deductive argument, *whenever the conclusion is false, at least one premise must be false as well.* **If there is ever an instance where the conclusion is false while all of the premises are true, then the argument is invalid.** It is for these conditions that we examine our truth table by following these steps:

Steps for Utilizing the Long Truth Table Method

1. **Construct a truth table that fully diagrams the argument to be tested for validity.**
   - Follow the rules for truth table formation in chapter 2. Use the contents of chapters 3 and 4 to determine the truth values of complex statements and symbolize complicated statements with brackets.
2. **Identify each row where the conclusion is false.**
   - Simply ignore rows in which the conclusion is true.
3. **Read across each row where the conclusion is false to check the truth of the premises.**
   - If you find a single instance where the **conclusion is false and all of the premises are true**, then you have an **invalid** argument.
   - If there is no such row, the argument is valid.

As you can see, our example argument is valid. The conclusion is false in rows 1 and 3. In each of those rows, at least one premise is false (Premise 1 in the first row and Premise 2 in the third row). This is really all there is to the long truth table method for checking validity: you have been developing many of the required skills to do this throughout the previous chapters in this book.

The truth table shows us all of the possible combinations of truth and falsity in the argument. (Notice that we're not yet concerned with the *actual* truth values of the premises.) Once we know a given deductive argument is valid, we still need to assess its soundness by determining the actual truth value of the premises; the above argument is always valid, but it's only sound if it is *actually* Thursday when the argument is made. And it is only when an argument is sound that the conclusion is actually supported by the premises and so should be accepted as true. This assessment of soundness is *not* something that truth tables can assist us with. However, by showing us that an argument is valid or invalid, the truth table method helps us determine whether or not it is worth our time to judge if the relevant premises are true or false.

Let's look at a more complex example. Here is another argument:

> "Yoda is not in the basement. If Yoda isn't in the basement, she must be either taking a nap or in the garden. So she must be either taking a nap or in the garden."

First, we need to translate this argument. The result is this:

> P = "Yoda is in the basement."
> Q = "Yoda is taking a nap."
> R = "Yoda is in the garden."

Next, we need to add our logical operators to provide a full symbolic representation of the argument. The result is this:

> 1. $-P$
> 2. $-P \rightarrow (Q \vee R)$
> 3. $\therefore Q \vee R$

This argument is interesting because the conclusion presents us a range of possibilities, namely Q or R. We have translated the "or" as an inclusive disjunction; as noted in section 4.2, Yoda can be taking a nap in the garden, so both Q and R can be true at the same time. Now we can construct a truth table to fully explore the possible truth conditions of all of the variables:

			Premise 1	Conclusion	Premise 2
P	Q	R	–P	Q v R	–P → (Q v R)
T	T	T	F	T	T
T	T	F	F	T	T
T	F	T	F	T	T
T	F	F	F	F	T
F	T	T	T	T	T
F	T	F	T	T	T
F	F	T	T	T	T
F	F	F	T	F	F

Now analyze the truth table for validity. Identify all rows in which the conclusion is false and then check each row to see if at least one premise is false. Pause reading now and do that.

The conclusion is false in rows 4 and 8. Premise 1 is false in row 4. Premise 2 is false in row 8. So there are no rows where the conclusion is false and all of the premises are true. It looks like we have identified another valid argument.

Before concluding this chapter, let's test an invalid argument using the long truth table method. We will test this invalid argument introduced above: "Either it is raining or it is snowing. It is raining. So it is snowing." We can symbolize that argument as follows:

R = "It is raining."
S = "It is snowing."
1. R v S
2. R
3. ∴ S

Here is the truth table for this argument:

Premise 2	Conclusion	Premise 1
R	S	R v S
T	T	T
T	F	T
F	T	T
F	F	F

To check the argument for validity, we check each row where the conclusion is false. In this argument, the conclusion is false in rows 2 and 4. In row 4 we see that both premises are false. However, in row 2, we see that both premises are true while the conclusion is false. Because we have found an instance where the premises can be true and the conclusion is false, this table shows us that this argument is invalid, i.e., the truth of the premises does not guarantee the truth of the conclusion.

That is all there is to the long truth table method. Following the same basic procedure, you can check the validity of any deductive argument, no matter how long. The main disadvantage of the long truth table method is that it can be very time-consuming to use in assessing a long argument. To expedite this process, we may instead utilize the short truth table method. We will turn our attention to it in the next chapter.

5.3   Practice Questions

1. What relationship holds between the premises and conclusion of a formally valid deductive argument?
2. What does it mean for a deductive argument to be sound?

Test the following arguments for validity using the long truth table method. Explain why the argument is valid or invalid. If the argument is invalid, identify which row(s) prove that it is invalid:

3. 1. P & Q
   2. P → R
   3. ∴ R

4. 1. P v Q
   2. P → R
   3. ∴ R

5. 1. −P
   2. P v Q
   3. ∴ Q

6. 1. −P
   2. −P v Q
   3. ∴ Q

7. 1. P → Q
   2. −Q & −R
   3. ∴ P

8. 1. (P v Q) & R
   2. R → −Q
   3. ∴ P

9. 1. P → Q
   2. Q → R
   3. −P
   4. ∴ P → R

10. 1. P → (Q v R)
    2. P → −Q
    3. P
    4. ∴ R

11. 1. −(P & Q) v R
    2. R → P
    3. ∴ −Q

12. 1. P v −Q
    2. R → Q
    3. −P
    4. ∴ −R

CHAPTER 6

The Short Truth Table Method

6.1   Steps for Using the Short Truth Table Method
6.2   Examples of the Short Truth Table Method
6.3   Practice Questions

Once you have a firm grasp of how the long truth table method works, you may use the short truth table method to save time. The long method exhaustively explores all of the possible combinations of truth values for the logical units that make up an argument. The short method tries to simply find an instance of invalidity in an argument. It achieves this aim by assuming that the conclusion is false and then checking if all of the premises can be true without encountering a contradiction. If we can achieve that result, then we know that the argument is invalid. If we are unable to make the conclusion false while all the premises are true, then we have a valid argument on our hands. We will work through examples of how to use this method below, but first let's explain how to use it.

6.1 Steps for Using the Short Truth Table Method

When using the short truth table method, follow these steps:

1. **Create the header row for a truth table that represents the argument and add a single row under the header row.**
    • Follow the steps in section 2.2 to create the header row.

- Remember to include a separate column for each simple statement and complex statement in the argument.
- Label the premises and the conclusion in the header row.

2. **Set the conclusion to false.**
   - If the conclusion is a complex statement, then also fill in the truth values of the logical units included in the conclusion.
   - If there is more than one way for the conclusion to be false, start by arbitrarily making it false in one of the ways possible.
   - For example, if the conclusion is a conjunction, then it will be false when either, or both, of the conjuncts are false. Make the conjunction false and make one, or both, conjuncts false; it does not matter which conjunct(s) you make false, as long as the conclusion is false.

3. **Begin setting premises to true.**
   Now that the conclusion is false, try to make all of the premises true without contradicting yourself. If you encounter an instance where you are forced to make a premise false, then mark it as false and stop filling in this row. Follow these steps in setting premises to true:

   a. **Set the truth value of all premises that are simple statements to true.**

   b. **Set the truth value of all premises that are negated simple statements to true.**
      - If a simple statement is true, its negation must be false, and vice versa. When you have a statement and its negation on a truth table, you can fill in the values for both as soon as you know the value for one of them, keeping in mind that they will always have opposite truth values in a given row (i.e., if the statement is true its negation is false and vice versa).

   c. **Set the truth value of all premises that are conjunctions to true.**
      - Remember that when a conjunction is true, both conjuncts must be true. Fill in the values for the conjuncts as well.

- If a conjunction contains a complex statement other than another conjunction or negation as a conjunct, do not set the conjunction's truth value to true yet.

d. **Set the truth value of all premises that are *negated* inclusive disjunctions and *negated* implications to true.**
   - If an inclusive disjunction is false, both disjuncts must be false. Fill in the values for both disjuncts.
   - When an implication statement is false, its antecedent must be true while its consequent is false. Fill in the values for the antecedent and consequent.

e. **Set the truth values of all remaining premises to true.**
   - Because the simple statements in true inclusive disjunctions, true implication statements, and biconditional statements can have varying truth values, we deal with those types of operators last.
   - When trying to set such premises to true, consult the truth values you have already set for simple statements in the argument.

   If at any point you reach a contradiction, immediately move on to step 4. You reach a contradiction if you need to set the truth value of a statement to both true and false in order to be consistent with the other truth values entered on the table.

4. **Assess the table.**

   a. If on any row you manage to set the truth value of all the premises in the argument to true while the conclusion is false, and you do not contradict yourself, **then the argument is invalid**.

   b. Otherwise, ask whether there is any remaining way in which the conclusion could be false. If there is, add a new row to the table and return to step 2. If a conclusion is a simple statement, or a negated simple statement, negated disjunction, or negated implication statement, there is only one way for it to be false. Conclusions that include a disjunction, conjunction, implication, or biconditional statement will have more than one way of being false.

c. If neither a) nor b) applies—that is, if you've constructed enough rows to exhaust all possible ways that the conclusion can be false without reaching a contradiction—**then the argument is valid**.

When applying steps 2 and 3 of the short truth table method, be sure to keep these important points in mind:

- Whenever you have enough information to fill in a truth value, do so. E.g., If you set a simple statement to true, and because that simple statement is true an inclusive disjunction containing that simple statement is true, make the inclusive disjunction true as well.
- Simply stop constructing a row if you are ever forced to contradict yourself by setting the same statement to both true and false. If setting a premise to true would result in a contradiction, set it to false instead and then stop constructing the row. If you cannot make all of the premises true while the conclusion is false, then the row cannot show invalidity, so we need not waste our time filing out a whole row if we know at least one premise will be false in that row.

6.2 Examples of the Short Truth Table Method

Example #1:

Let's begin by testing an example argument used in the previous chapter to illustrate the use of the short truth table technique: "if it's Thursday, then it's not Tuesday. It's Thursday, so it must not be Tuesday." We translate that to:

P = "It is Thursday."
Q = "It is Tuesday."

Next, we symbolize the argument:

1. $P \rightarrow -Q$
2. P
3. $\therefore -Q$

We are now in a position to construct a truth table. However, instead of creating 2^n rows (which would be four rows in this case), we simply start with our header row (which contains all of our statements, as well as labels for the premises and the conclusion) and one row where we set the conclusion to false. Our table will look like this after we have completed steps 1 and 2 above:

Premise 2		Conclusion	Premise 1
P	Q	−Q	P → −Q
		F	

Because the conclusion −Q is false, we know that Q must be true. Let's fill that in next:

Premise 2		Conclusion	Premise 1
P	Q	−Q	P → −Q
	T	F	

Now our aim is to try to make all of the premises true while the conclusion is false. Following step 3, we start with premises containing simple statements. In this argument, that's Premise 2:

Premise 2		Conclusion	Premise 1
P	Q	−Q	P → −Q
T	T	F	

The reason we make Premise 2 true before making Premise 1 true in this instance is because Premise 2 is a simple statement (the statement P).

We can now fill in the value of Premise 1 by consulting the first and third columns: the antecedent is true (T), and the consequent is false (F), making Premise 1 F. For the argument to be invalid there has to be at least one row with T premises and a F conclusion. But we've just shown that when the conclusion is F and Premise 2 is T, Premise 1 is F. So it's impossible for there to be a row where both premises are T and the conclusion is F. The argument is valid.

Since there is only one way for the conclusion to be false, we only need a single row to conclude that **this argument is valid**.

We've quadrupled our efficiency compared to using the long truth table method because we only had to construct one row instead of four to test this argument for validity.

Remember, though: if there is more than one way for the conclusion of an argument to be false, then we *may* have to construct multiple rows on our table. As soon as we find a single instance of invalidity we may stop constructing rows, because we have found what we are looking for. If we do not find invalidity, then we construct a row for each possible way in which the conclusion might be false. If we have made every such possible row, but are unable to find an instance of invalidity, then we have shown the argument to be valid.

Example #2:

1. −P
2. −P → (Q v R)
3. ∴ Q & R

The first two steps of the short truth table method will give us this:

			Premise 1		Premise 2	Conclusion
P	Q	R	−P	Q v R	−P → (Q v R)	Q & R
						F

We have made the conclusion Q & R false. Recall that a conjunction is only true when *both* the conjuncts are true. That means that Q & R is false when Q, R, or both Q and R are false. Because the conclusion can be false in three possible ways, we have up to three rows to check on our table. We will stop once we find any row in which the conclusion is false and the premises true (without contradiction), or after we have checked each of the three rows. Let's start by arbitrarily making Q true and R false:

			Premise 1		Premise 2	Conclusion
P	Q	R	–P	Q v R	–P → (Q v R)	Q & R
	T	F				F

Now we know that Q v R is true because Q is true:

			Premise 1		Premise 2	Conclusion
P	Q	R	–P	Q v R	–P → (Q v R)	Q & R
	T	F		T		F

There is one more cell value we can fill in at this point. We already know that Q v R is true. An implication statement is true whenever its consequent is true, and Q v R is the consequent of the implication statement in the second premise:

			Premise 1		Premise 2	Conclusion
P	Q	R	–P	Q v R	–P → (Q v R)	Q & R
	T	F		T	T	F

Now the only thing left to do to complete this truth table is to see if we can make the remaining premise true without contradicting ourselves. Premise 1 is a negated simple statement, and it will be true if P is false. Looking at our truth table, there is no reason why we cannot set −P to true (and P to false). Doing so produces no contradiction, so let's do that now:

			Premise 1	Premise 2		Conclusion
P	**Q**	**R**	**−P**	**Q v R**	**−P → (Q v R)**	**Q & R**
F	T	F	T	T	T	F

In this row we have set the premises as true and the conclusion as false, without contradiction. We have thus demonstrated that **the argument is invalid**, so we may stop without having to check the other two possible rows.

Example #3:

Let's try one more example case to see the full power of the short method. We will use this argument:

> 1. P
> 2. −Q
> 3. Q v R
> 4. R → S
> 5. ∴ P & (R & S)

The conclusion of this argument is a conjunction that includes another conjunction as one of the conjuncts. The conclusion states that P, R, and S are all true, so that complex statement is false if any one of those three simple statements is false. Although you may be able to look at this argument and see that it is indeed valid, we will use the short truth table method to demonstrate that fact. We start with this:

Premise 1				Premise 2	Premise 3	Premise 4		Conclusion
P	Q	R	S	−Q	Q v R	R → S	R & S	P & (R & S)
								F

Because there are three ways for the conclusion to be false, we will set the truth values of the simple statements contained in it in such a way that the conclusion is false. We will also set P and −Q (and Q as a result) to true because they are given to us as premises:

Premise 1				Premise 2	Premise 3	Premise 4		Conclusion
P	Q	R	S	−Q	Q v R	R → S	R & S	P & (R & S)
T	F	F	F	T				F

Here we have set both R and S to false which makes the conclusion false. Now we must see if we can set our other premises to true and not contradict ourselves:

Premise 1				Premise 2	Premise 3	Premise 4		Conclusion
P	Q	R	S	−Q	Q v R	R → S	R & S	P & (R & S)
T	F	F	F	T	F			F

We've hit a dead end. Premise 3 must be false because both Q and R are false, so Q v R must be false as well. Given that we know that Q must be false because −Q is true, let's make a second row where we set R to true and leave S as false to ensure our conclusion is still false:

Premise 1				Premise 2	Premise 3	Premise 4		Conclusion
P	Q	R	S	–Q	Q v R	R → S	R & S	P & (R & S)
T	F	F	F	T	F			F
T	F	T	F	T				F

Because R is true, we can set premise 3 to true in this row:

Premise 1				Premise 2	Premise 3	Premise 4		Conclusion
P	Q	R	S	–Q	Q v R	R → S	R & S	P & (R & S)
T	F	F	F	T	F			F
T	F	T	F	T	T			F

Now if we can make premise 4 true without contradicting ourselves, we will have shown this argument to be invalid. Can we do that? No, we cannot, because R is true while S is false, and that makes the implication statement R → S false as well. We can enter that value on our truth table:

Premise 1				Premise 2	Premise 3	Premise 4		Conclusion
P	Q	R	S	–Q	Q v R	R → S	R & S	P & (R & S)
T	F	F	F	T	F			F
T	F	T	F	T	T	F		F

At this point, we know that this argument is valid. We cannot make the conclusion false by making P false because P must be true as a premise to demonstrate that the argument is invalid. We know that R must be true to make Q v R true because −Q is true as a premise. Lastly, we know that S must be true because we know R must be true, and R → S must be true as a premise to demonstrate invalidity. Here is the full short truth table that includes the other possible ways the conclusion can be false, stopping where at least one premise must be set to false to avoid contradiction:

Premise 1				Premise 2	Premise 3	Premise 4		Conclusion
P	Q	R	S	−Q	Q v R	R → S	R & S	P & (R & S)
T	F	F	F	T	F			F
T	F	T	F	T	T	F		F
T	F	F	T	T	F			F
F		T	T					F
F		F	T					F
F		T	F					F

As you can see, only having to write out a few rows is much faster than completing every row, although the process is less mechanical.[10] Remember, we must construct rows to check each way an argument may be invalid *until* we find an instance of invalidity *or* until we have exhausted all possible ways the conclusion may be false. However, we only need to find one instance of invalidity for the argument to be invalid.

---

10. In the web supplement, we present an argument whose full truth table requires a large number of rows, and walk you through the shorter method for showing validity.

6.3 Practice Questions

Test the following arguments for validity using the short truth table method:

1. 1. P → Q
    2. −Q
    3. ∴ −P

2. 1. P & Q
    2. Q → R
    3. ∴ R

3. 1. P v Q
    2. P → R
    3. ∴ Q

4. 1. −(P v Q)
    2. −Q v R
    3. ∴ −R

5. 1. (P & Q) → R
    2. −(−P v −Q)
    3. ∴ R

6. 1. (P v Q) & (R v S)
    2. P → −S
    3. −Q
    4. ∴ R

7. 1. (P v Q) & R
    2. R → −Q
    3. ∴ P

8. 1. P v Q
    2. Q → R
    3. R → S
    4. −P
    5. ∴ S v T

9. 1. (P & Q) → R
    2. P v S
    3. −S
    4. Q & T
    5. ∴ R

10. 1. −P
    2. Q → R
    3. P v Q
    4. ∴ Q & R

PART III

Demonstrating Validity with Proofs

CHAPTER 7

Valid and Invalid Argument Forms

7.1 *Modus ponens*
7.2 *Modus tollens*
7.3 Hypothetical Syllogism (chain argument)
7.4 Disjunctive Syllogism
7.5 Invalid Argument Form: Affirming the Consequent
7.6 Invalid Argument Form: Denying the Antecedent
7.7 Practice Questions

Now that we have a firm understanding of logical operators and truth tables, we can familiarize ourselves with some of the most common valid and invalid argument forms. As the names imply, valid argument forms are particular structures of deductive reasoning that are always valid, no matter the particular content contained within that argument form. Invalid argument forms are always invalid, regardless of their particular content. Below are brief explanations of some of these forms and their associated truth tables to demonstrate in what way the forms are valid or invalid.

7.1 *Modus ponens*

The name "*modus ponens*" is Latin and translates, roughly, to "the way that affirms." A *modus ponens* argument is one that affirms an implication statement and affirms the antecedent of that statement. For example:

1. If I am studying logic, then I am a very intelligent person.
2. I am studying logic.
3. Therefore, I am a very intelligent person.

Translation:
P = "I am studying logic."
Q = "I am a very intelligent person."

When we affirm the implication statement and its antecedent, we must then affirm its consequent as well. We can see this clearly on the truth table, which mimics the truth table of implication itself:

Premise 2	Conclusion	Premise 1
P	Q	P $\rightarrow$ Q
T	T	T
T	F	F
F	T	T
F	F	T

We see in rows 2 and 4 that, each time the conclusion is false, at least one premise is false as well. *Modus ponens*, like the other rules for valid arguments discussed below, is truth preserving.[11] Whenever you identify an argument that is simply the *modus ponens* form, you can immediately conclude that you are dealing with a valid argument structure.

7.2   Modus tollens

Another valid argument form centred on implication statements is *modus tollens*, which roughly translates to "the way that denies." It is

---

11. You might want to look again at what "truth preserving" means. It was discussed in part 5.1.

helpful to think of modus tollens as the valid, reverse form of modus ponens: whereas modus ponens affirms the antecedent of an affirmed implication statement, and thus validly affirms the consequent as a result, a modus tollens argument denies the consequent of an affirmed implication statement, and thus denies the antecedent as a result. Here is an example of modus tollens:

1. If I am studying logic, then I am a very intelligent person.
2. I am not a very intelligent person.
3. Therefore, I am not studying logic.

Translation:
P = "I am studying logic."
Q = "I am a very intelligent person."

	Conclusion		Premise 2	Premise 1
P	–P	Q	–Q	P → Q
T	F	T	F	T
T	Г	F	T	F
F	T	T	F	T
F	T	F	T	T

We have added columns to include the negation of P and Q, as they are included in our second premise and conclusion. As you can see from the truth table, this argument form is valid. By accepting the implication statement P → Q, we are claiming that whenever P is true Q must be true as well. That means that if Q is false, P must also be false (although Q may be true when P is false). Look at rows 1 and 2 of the truth table where our conclusion (–P) is false. We see in those rows that at least one premise is false whenever the conclusion is false; in other words, we see that it is impossible that all premises be true while the conclusion is false (i.e., there is no row representing this). Hence, we have another valid argument form.

7.3   Hypothetical Syllogism (chain argument)

Hypothetical syllogisms deal with how two implication statements connect with one another. The connection is complicated to describe but easy to see. It's of this form:

$$1. P \rightarrow Q$$
$$2. Q \rightarrow R$$
$$3. \therefore P \rightarrow R$$

Here is an example of hypothetical syllogism:

1. If the United States launches a strike at North Korea, then North Korea attacks South Korea.
2. If North Korea attacks South Korea, then thousands of South Koreans will be killed.
3. Therefore, if the United States launches a strike at North Korea, then thousands of South Koreans will be killed.

Translation:
P = The United States launches a strike at North Korea.
Q = North Korea attacks South Korea.
R = Thousands of South Koreans will be killed.

Let's look at the truth table for this argument:

			Premise 1	Premise 2	Conclusion
P	Q	R	P → Q	Q → R	P → R

As we can see on the next page, this argument is valid. The conclusion is false only in rows 2 and 4, and in those rows at least one premise is always false (Premise 1 in row 4, Premise 2 in row 2). Hypothetical syllogisms are useful ways of condensing complex relations into far more efficient forms. They are often also called "chain arguments" because they "chain" together implication statements.

			Premise 1	Premise 2	Conclusion
P	Q	R	P→Q	Q→R	P→R
T	T	T	T	T	T
T	T	F	T	F	F
T	F	T	F	T	T
T	F	F	F	T	F
F	T	T	T	T	T
F	T	F	T	F	T
F	F	T	T	T	T
F	F	F	T	T	T

7.4 Disjunctive Syllogism

Disjunctive syllogisms are two-premise arguments that contain one disjunctive statement and a premise that denies one of the disjuncts. The conclusion of the disjunctive syllogism is that the remaining disjunct is true. For example:

1. Either Kareem will bring donuts or Liam will bring cupcakes.
2. Kareem will not bring donuts.
3. Therefore, Liam will bring cupcakes.
Translation:
P = "Kareem will bring donuts."
Q = "Liam will bring cupcakes."

Symbolic argument:
1. P v Q
2. –P
3. ∴ Q

Let's examine the truth table for this argument:

	Premise 2	*Conclusion*	*Premise 1*
P	**−P**	**Q**	**P v Q**
T	F	T	T
T	F	F	T
F	T	T	T
F	T	F	F

As we can see from rows 2 and 4, at least one premise is always false when the conclusion is false (Premise 2 in row 2, Premise 1 in row 4), making this argument valid. Note that, while we made the first disjunct false in this example, it does not matter which disjunct is false for a disjunctive syllogism to be valid.

7.5 Invalid Argument Form: Affirming the Consequent

While *modus ponens* is a valid argument form, there is a closely related invalid argument form that resembles *modus ponens*. That argument form is affirming the consequent. Consider this argument:

1. If I am studying logic, then I am a very intelligent person.
2. I am a very intelligent person.
3. Therefore, I am studying logic.

Translation:
P = "I am studying logic."
Q = "I am a very intelligent person."

Affirming the consequent occurs when an implication statement is accepted, its consequent is affirmed, and its antecedent is affirmed as a conclusion. We can see this on a truth table:

Conclusion	Premise 2	Premise 1
P	Q	P → Q
T	T	T
T	F	F
F	T	T
F	F	T

As you can see from row 3, this is an invalid argument form. Both premises may be true while the conclusion (in this case P, the antecedent) is false. Because each implication statement only captures a unidirectional relationship from antecedent to consequent, we are not allowed to infer "backwards" through the argument from consequent to antecedent.

7.6 Invalid Argument Form: Denying the Antecedent

There is another invalid argument form related to implication statements. This form is denying the antecedent. Denying the antecedent occurs when we accept an implication statement, deny the antecedent, and deny the consequent as a result. Using our example once again, with the appropriate modifications

> 1. If I am studying logic, then I am a very intelligent person.
> 2. I am not studying logic.
> 3. Therefore, I am not a very intelligent person.

> Translation:
> P = "I am studying logic."
> Q = "I am a very intelligent person."

	Premise 2		Conclusion		Premise 1
P	–P	Q	–Q	P → Q
T	F	T	F	T
T	F	F	T	F
F	T	T	F	T
F	T	F	T	T

Examine row 3. There you will see that this argument form is invalid because the conclusion is false while both premises are true. The implication statement tells us that, if the antecedent is true, the consequent must be true. Recall that this relationship is unidirectional; the implication statement says nothing about what must be the case when the antecedent is false. The consequent may be true for a host of reasons besides the truth of the antecedent.

7.7 Practice Questions

Translate and symbolize the following arguments. Identify what kind of argument form(s) each argument contains and whether or not the argument is valid as a result.

1. Either Sally will come to the party or Jason will come to the party, but not both (because they hate each other). Jason said he won't come to the party, so Sally must be coming to the party.

2. Whenever it rains my roof leaks, and every time my roof leaks my carpet gets wet. So every time it rains my carpet gets wet.

3. If Karl wrote a logic text, he must be a very cool person. But Karl is not a very cool person, so he must not have written a logic text.

4. If Neta proofreads a friend's writing, then she must be a good friend. Neta did proofread a friend's writing, so she must be a good friend.

5. When Ruthann plays video games she has fun. And when Ruthann is having fun she is happy. So, Ruthann is happy when she plays video games.

6. If Xi wins the race, then he must be a fast runner. Xi didn't win the race, so he must be slow.

7. Whenever it rains I take my umbrella with me. I have my umbrella, so it must be raining.

8. Either Shelly or Jim will get the job, and if Jim gets the job then I will get a raise. Shelly won't get the job, so I'll get a raise.

9. When people annoy Jennifer, she gets either angry or quiet. Jennifer is angry, so people must be annoying her.

10. Either Alex vacationed in Paris or Vancouver last summer. If he vacationed in Paris he must have seen the Eiffel Tower, but he hasn't seen it, so he must have been in Vancouver.

Proofs

8.1 The Method of Proofs

A proof attempts to show that a given argument is valid by taking the argument's premises and attempting to work in a step-by-step manner to reach the argument's conclusion. Proofs utilize **rules of inference** in their steps. These rules represent valid argument structures. Knowing that each rule is valid ensures that, if we can reach the conclusion using only the rules and the argument's premises, then the argument itself is valid.

If we compare proofs to chess (or a similar game), the rules of inference are the moves we're allowed to make. We win the "game" of proofs by reaching the conclusion without cheating (i.e., by only making moves that the rules allow us to make). Because proof techniques resemble our normal reasoning, they are often referred to as "natural deduction." This chapter will explain how to read and write proofs, and examine the rules of inference. Proofs may also use **logical equivalents** in their steps. Logical equivalents allow us to rewrite part of a proof by substituting one statement for another with the same truth conditions. Chapter 10 will explore logical equivalents.

8.2 How to Read and Write Proofs

A proof begins by providing an argument's premises and indicating what conclusion is supposed to be proven true from those premises. The conclusion is written to the right of the last premise. For example:

> 1. P
> 2. P → Q   ∴ Q

The reason that we do not give the conclusion a line of its own when writing out a proof is because we add additional lines to the argument when completing a proof. Each line involves a "move" as described above, i.e., the application of a rule of inference or logical equivalent used to advance the argument towards the conclusion. We have completed the proof when we successfully reach the conclusion. If we cannot reach the conclusion by following the rules of inference, that failure by itself does not show that the argument is invalid; all it shows is that we have failed to construct a proof. One major shortcoming of using proofs is that they cannot demonstrate when an argument is invalid. To show that an argument is invalid, one of the truth table methods explained in earlier chapters must be used.

With each step we take in constructing a proof, we write out a new line and indicate which statements and rules we've used in the process. By now you probably realize that our example argument is a simple *modus ponens*. We can complete our proof by adding a single line:

> 1. P
> 2. P → Q   ∴ Q
> 3. Q   1, 2, MP

Line three reads as follows: we attain Q from lines 1 and 2 by applying *modus ponens* (represented by the shorthand "MP"). We will simply end our proof when we have stated the desired conclusion in a line. Below, we will examine the rules of inference, seeing why they work (via truth tables) and how they work (in some example arguments).

8.3 Rules of Inference

Here is a list of valid rules of inference, with the abbreviations we'll use from now on. The first four of which are simply the valid argument forms discussed in chapter 7:

Rule name (shorthand symbols)	Rule function (in symbolic form)
Modus Ponens (MP)	$P \rightarrow Q$ P $\therefore Q$
Modus Tollens (MT)	$P \rightarrow Q$ $-Q$ $\therefore -P$
Hypothetical (Chain) Syllogism (HS)	$P \rightarrow Q$ $Q \rightarrow R$ $\therefore P \rightarrow R$
Disjunctive Syllogism (DS)	$P \lor Q$ $P \lor Q$ $-P$ *or* $-Q$ $\therefore Q$ $\therefore P$
Addition (Add)	P P $\therefore P \lor Q$ *or* $\therefore Q \lor P$
Simplification (Simp)	$P \& Q$ $P \& Q$ $\therefore P$ *or* $\therefore Q$
Conjunction Introduction (Conj)	P Q $\therefore P \& Q$
Constructive Dilemma (CD)	$(P \rightarrow Q) \& (R \rightarrow S)$ $P \lor R$ $\therefore Q \lor S$
Reiteration (R)	P $\therefore P$

In the left column are the names and abbreviations of the rules. In the right column is a representation of each rule's function. To apply a rule, you must have certain "inputs" to produce the desired "output." The inputs are provided here as premises and the outputs as conclusions.[12] For example, in the first rule (MP), we have two inputs, P → Q and P, followed by Q, which is the output they allow us to reach. While specific letters have been used here for example purposes, it is important to note that these rules apply in the same way to any set of logical units, so long as the pattern presented here is consistently followed. For instance, one does not need a "P" and "Q" to apply MP, but we can apply MP to any two logical units. Here are a few examples of how we may apply MP:

R → T	(P & Q) → R	(P v Q) → (−S & T)
R	P & Q	P v Q
∴ T	∴ R	∴ −S & T

But this is a mistaken use of MP:

$$P \lor (Q \rightarrow R)$$
$$Q$$
$$\therefore P \lor R$$

It is mistaken because it attempts to apply the rule to an implication (Q → R) which is "inside" a larger statement. To use MP, the implication statement, as well as the statement of the antecedent and the conclusion—the consequent—must each be whole lines.

Recall that the first four rules of inference were explained in chapter 7. We can use them to show validity because we know that their application always preserves the truth of lines above them, thus their use will always result in lines validly derivable from the assumptions of the argument. Let's now examine the five new rules so see what they allow us to do in a proof. Keep in mind that P and Q will be used for

---

12. You can think of each application of a rule of inference as a subargument, with the inputs acting as premises and the outputs as conclusions. These subarguments ultimately drive the argument toward the main conclusion.

explanatory purposes, but these rules function in the same way for any logical units we may substitute in place of P or Q.

Addition (Add)

P or P

∴ P v Q ∴ Q v P

The rule of addition tells us that if P is true, then any disjunction that contains P is true as well. This means that we can formulate the disjunction P v Q whenever we are given P and retain validity. Recall the disjunction truth table: the truth of one disjunct is sufficient for the truth of the whole disjunction.

While creating a disjunction in this way may seem like a form of cheating because we are adding any disjunct we like, just remember that the disjunction must be true as long as at least one disjunct is true.

Here is an example of this rule in natural language: "Yoda enjoys eating treats. So, either Yoda enjoys eating treats or she enjoys going to the vet." Because it's true that Yoda enjoys eating treats, any disjunction that features that statement as one of its disjuncts is automatically true, no matter the truth or falsity of the second disjunct.

Simplification (Simp)

P & Q or P & Q

∴ P ∴ Q

The rule of simplification tells us that, if P & Q is true, then each of P and Q are true on their own. We simplify the conjunction by removing one of its parts, leaving us with one of the two original conjuncts. When P & Q is true, both P and Q are true, making simplification a valid rule of inference.

Note that when you simplify a conjunction, you can assert that either the first or second conjunct is true. However, you must apply the rule each time you wish to assert that one of the conjuncts is true, i.e., you require a separate line in the proof each time you wish to apply simplification, and each application of simplification will only allow you to assert that one conjunct is true.

Here is a natural language example of simplification: "Karl is writing a logic book and Karl has sideburns. So, Karl is writing a logic book." Here is another one: "Karl is writing a logic book and Karl has sideburns. So, Karl has sideburns."

Conjunction Introduction (Conj)

P

Q

∴ P & Q

The rule of conjunction introduction is the partner rule to simplification. If we know that two statements, such as P and Q, are each true, then the complex statement P & Q must be true as well. Note that the order of the two statements to be conjoined need not be the same as in the conjunction. This sort of argument is legitimate also:

P

Q

∴ Q & P

In natural language, we can simply reverse our previous example. If we know that "Karl is writing a logic book" and "Karl has sideburns" are both true, then we can validly assert the conjunction "Karl is writing a logic book and Karl has sideburns." Those premises also allow us to assert the conjunction "Karl has sideburns and he is writing a logic book."

Constructive Dilemma (CD)

(P → Q) & (R → S)

P v R

∴ Q v S

This is the most complex rule, but there is some intuitive sense to it. We use the constructive dilemma when we think about possibilities and potential results. A constructive dilemma is composed of three parts: a disjunction, which tells us that (at least) one of two things will happen, and two implication statements that track the possible consequences that will occur when either of those disjuncts is true. The conclusion we can derive from this scenario is that one or the other consequence will be true. Here's a natural language example: tomorrow morning I'll either go for a long walk or sleep in. If I go for a long walk, then I'll get some exercise, and if I sleep in then I'll be well rested. So, tomorrow morning either I'll get some exercise or I'll be well rested.

Note that the constructive dilemma uses an inclusive disjunction, so in the example just provided it must be possible to both go for a long walk and sleep in.

Reiteration

P

∴ P

Reiteration is a very simple rule. It allows us to simply restate whatever is already present in an argument on one line in another, subsequent line of the proof. Applying reiteration on its own will rarely move you closer to completing a proof, but it is a useful rule to use in long, complicated proofs so that you can organize information within the proof.

8.4 Applying the Rules of Inference

Now let's take a brief look at how we apply these rules of inference to complete a proof. We'll start with some simple examples.

Example #1:

We have already seen how to read and write a proof and how to apply the rules of inference. Building upon what you've learned so far, try to complete the following proof before reading the explanation of how to do it below. Here's one tip: you'll need to use two different rules of inference:

1. P

2. P → Q   ∴ P & Q

Just by seeing the two premises, you may have quickly reached for MP (*modus ponens*) because you saw its pattern in the premises. Let's apply that rule now:

1. P
2. P → Q   ∴ P & Q
3. Q   1, 2, MP

On the third line we apply MP. We write out the result we get, which is Q, and to the right of that result we write out the line(s) and rule we used to attain it. We read the content to the right of Q as "applying MP to lines 1 and 2 results in Q."

As we can see, applying MP will not produce the conclusion we desire on its own, although we now have the inputs we need to reach the desired conclusion P & Q. To reach that conclusion, we also need to apply conjunction introduction:

1. P
2. P → Q   ∴ P & Q
3. Q   1, 2, MP
4. P & Q   1, 3, Conj

In line 4, we prove the conclusion we set out to prove by drawing on lines 1 and 3 and applying the rule of conjunction introduction. Remember, each line produced using a rule of inference preserves validity. If we can derive the argument's conclusion from the argument's premises using the rules of inference, then the argument as a whole is valid.

Example #2:

Let's take a look at one more fairly straightforward example before moving on to more complex proofs. This example will also require the application of two rules of inference. See if you can figure out which rules you will need to use before reading the explanation below (tip: they are different rules than what we used in the previous example):

1. P v –Q
2. R → Q
3. –P   ∴ –R

This proof will require us to use DS (disjunctive syllogism) and MT (*modus tollens*). In line 1 we have a disjunction and in line 3 one of those disjuncts is negated. We can apply DS to lines 1 and 3 and we will be left with the other disjunct. Here's how we do that:

1. P v –Q
2. R → Q
3. –P   ∴ –R
4. –Q   1, 3, DS

Once we have –Q, we can then do something with the implication statement on line 2. In this case we can apply MT because the consequent of that implication statement is denied. By applying MT, we can deny the antecedent as well, which will end our proof:

1. P v –Q
2. R → Q
3. –P   ∴ –R
4. –Q   1, 3, DS
5. –R   2, 4, MT

These examples show us how to complete proofs that are relatively easy. These examples are relatively easy because we can only solve them in one way, and there is a particular order in which we must apply the rules of inference to derive our desired conclusion. In the next section we will discuss some more complex cases where there are different ways of solving the proof.

8.5 Strategies for Approaching Proofs

What is most important to keep in mind is that what we are allowed to do in a proof is constrained by the rules we have at our disposal. Some rules we can apply almost whenever we want. For instance, we can always use Add (addition) to create a disjunction, Conj (conjunction introduction) to create a conjunction with two provided logical units, or Simp (simplification) to break two conjoined logical units apart. Here is an example of how we can go in circles in a proof without actually making any progress towards our desired conclusion:

1. P		
2. Q		
3. Q → R	∴ R	
4. P & Q	1, 2, Conj	
5. P	4, Simp	
6. Q	4, Simp	
7. P & Q	5, 6, Conj	
8. P v R	1, Add	
9. Q v R	2, Add	

What have we accomplished in this example? Nothing that gets us any closing to proving R! In fact, much of what we've done in this example is redundant. On lines 5 and 6 we derived P and Q, which we already had in our premises in lines 1 and 2. We haven't done anything technically wrong, because every move we made utilized a valid rule of inference.

So our first lesson is to keep our sights on what we desire to prove. Just like taking a journey somewhere, we want to make sure that we plan our movements in accordance with our ultimate goal. Completing a proof is in some ways like navigating a maze or completing a puzzle. It can be helpful to take a look at the whole thing in order to make sense of which small moves will help reach your goal. When first looking at a proof, it is useful to consider the following questions:

1. What are the premises?
2. What rules of inference can I apply to these premises? Do I see any patterns that allow for the valid application of certain rules?
3. What is the desired conclusion? Which rules will move me towards proving the conclusion?

When considering question three, keep in mind that as you apply the rules of inference to the premises, you will typically derive new information that you can then use to apply the rules in ways that you originally could not.

Example #3:

One other important thing to keep in mind is that some proofs admit of multiple valid solutions. Let's look at an example proof that admits of two different solutions:

$$1. P \rightarrow Q$$
$$2. Q \rightarrow R$$
$$3. P \qquad \therefore R$$

In the first solution, we apply MP twice, thus achieving our conclusion:

1. $P \rightarrow Q$		
2. $Q \rightarrow R$		
3. P	$\therefore R$	
4. Q	1, 3, MP	
5. R	2, 4, MP	

However, we could also use the two implication statements, use HS (hypothetical syllogism), and apply MP once for the same result:

1. P → Q	
2. Q → R	
3. P	∴ R
4. P → R	1, 2, HS
5. R	3, 4, MP

This argument lends itself to two proofs, each of which show that it is a valid argument. As long as we construct one proof that allows us to affirm the conclusion is true, we know that the argument is valid.

Example #4:

One useful strategy when approaching complex proofs is to try to work both forwards and backwards. When you look at the initial premises, consider what rules you can apply and how that will lead you towards the conclusion. If doing that does not reveal an obvious way to reach the conclusion, also try working backwards by asking yourself what rules might let you prove the conclusion, and what pieces of information beside the conclusion you require to reach it.

Here is a more complex argument that we can use when seeing how to work in both directions:

1. P & Q	
2. P → –R	
3. R v S	∴ S

Thinking forwards from the premises, we can see that we have a possible application of MP using line 2. In order to apply MP, we will need to affirm the antecedent P, which we have inside line 1. We can get P by simplifying the conjunction P & Q. Once we've done that, we'll have –R, which we can then use when applying DS to line 3.

Thinking backwards from the conclusion of this same argument, we can see that we need to get S out of R v S. The rule we can use to assert that one disjunct in a disjunction is true is DS. To apply DS, we need to show that one of the disjuncts is false. In this case, we want to assert S, so we need to deny R (i.e., we need to show that R is false, or

that −R is true). Line 2 tells us that −R is true if P is true. Do we see P
asserted as true anywhere? We do see that on line 1. So, if we can assert
that P is true from line 1, we can work our way back to the conclusion.
And we can assert that P is true by applying Simp to line 1. Once we
know this last fact, we can then apply our rules of inference in a step-
by-step fashion to arrive at the desired conclusion.

> 1. P & Q
> 2. P → −R
> 3. R v S ∴ S
> 4. P 1, Simp
> 5. −R 2, 4, MP
> 6. S 3, 5, DS

Example #5:

Let's look at one last example that is more complex than what we've seen
so far. You will probably need to work both forwards and backwards to
solve it. Before reading the solution below, try to come up with your
own solution. Don't worry if your solution does not follow the solution
provided exactly step-by-step. As long as you prove the conclusion by
using the provided information and only applying the rules of inference, you are approaching this problem correctly:

> 1. P
> 2. (P v Q) → R
> 3. S
> 4. (R & S) → −T
> 5. X → T ∴ −X

Arguments such as this are so complex that you may need to use a combination of forward- and backwards-thinking. The right strategy may
not leap out at you, so sometimes completing a proof can be accomplished through a little trial-and-error. Just remember that as long as
you only make a move when you correctly apply a rule of inference,
you can never do something technically wrong, though the moves you

make may be redundant or lead you away from the conclusion instead of closer toward it. Ideally we want our proofs to be as simple as possible, but it is more important to ensure that proofs are technically correct than it is to ensure that they are elegant in this way.

Here's one possible solution:

1. P	
2. (P v Q) → R	
3. S	
4. (R & S) → −T	
5. X → T	∴ −X
6. P v Q	1, Add
7. R	2, 6, MP
8. R & S	3, 7, Conj
9. −T	4, 8, MP
10. −X	5, 9, MT

We first turn P into the disjunction P v Q through addition on line 6. Because we can assert that P v Q is true, we may claim R is true from applying MP to lines 2 and 6. Because R and S are both true (shown on lines 7 and 3, respectively), the conjunction R & S is also true, which we show on line 8 by applying Conj. We again apply MP by affirming the implication statement ([R & S] → −T) and its antecedent (lines 4 and 8), which gives us −T. Finally, knowing that −T is true, we may apply MT to line 5, allowing us to conclude that −X is true.

What do you think about these two items? Are they correct proofs?

1. (P & Q) → R		1. P → Q	
2. Q	∴ R	2. P & R	∴ Q
3. Q → R	1, Simp	3. P	2, Simp
4. R	2, 3, MP	4. R	2, Simp
		5. Q	3, 1, MP

Step 3 in the attempted proof on the left is mistaken. It attempts to apply Simp to a logical unit that is part of a larger statement in step 1. Our rules can be applied only to whole statements.

On the right is a correct proof. One thing you may have noticed about it is that in line 5, the step numbers referred to for MP are not in numerical order ("1, 3"), even though all the proofs given above put justifying numbers in that order. This doesn't matter. Another peculiarity of this proof is that step 4, although a correct use of Simp and step 2, isn't necessary. 'R' isn't used for anything. This might have been omitted. Omission would make the proof more elegant, but that doesn't matter either. As mentioned above, we're after truth, not beauty. Putting in a lot of useless but correct steps might raise the suspicion that you don't know exactly what you're doing, but as long as every step is correct and you get to the conclusion, you will have produced a correct proof.

8.6 Practice Questions

The practice questions in this section are organized into categories. There is a category for each rule of inference with questions that only use one rule at a time. Start with those questions so that you get an intuitive sense of how to use each rule. Once you are comfortable with applying each rule on its own, then approach the questions in the last category that require you to use more than one rule to produce a proof. Answers to all these practice questions are found in the web supplement.

MP (*Modus Ponens*)

1. 1. $P \to Q$
   2. P $\therefore Q$

2. 1. $R \to S$
   2. R $\therefore S$

3. 1. $P \to Q$
   2. $Q \to R$
   3. P $\therefore R$

4. 1. $(P \& Q) \to R$
   2. $P \& Q$ $\therefore R$

5. 1. $P \to (Q \& R)$
   2. P $\therefore Q \& R$

6. 1. $P \to (Q \lor R)$
   2. P $\therefore Q \lor R$

7. 1. $(P \lor Q) \to (R \& {-}S)$
   2. $P \lor Q$ $\therefore R \& {-}S$

8. 1. $(P \lor Q) \to (R \& {-}S)$
   2. $(R \& {-}S) \to {-}(T \lor U)$
   3. $P \lor Q$ $\therefore {-}(T \lor U)$

MT (*Modus Tollens*)

9. 1. P → Q
    2. –Q   ∴ –P

10. 1. R → S
    2. –S   ∴ –R

11. 1. P → Q
    2. Q → R
    3. –R   ∴ –P

12. 1. (P & Q) → R
    2. –R   ∴ –(P & Q)

13. 1. P → (Q & R)
    2. –(Q & R)   ∴ –P

14. 1. P → (Q v R)
    2. –(Q v R)   ∴ –P

15. 1. (P v Q) → (R & –S)
    2. –(R & –S)   ∴ –(P v Q)

DS (Disjunctive Syllogism)

16. 1. P v Q
    2. –Q   ∴ P

17. 1. P v Q
    2. –P   ∴ Q

18. 1. (P & Q) v R
    2. –R   ∴ P & Q

19. 1. (P & Q) v R
    2. –(P & Q)   ∴ R

20. 1. P v (Q & R)
    2. –(Q & R)   ∴ P

21. 1. P v (Q & R)
    2. –P   ∴ Q & R

22. 1. (P v Q) v (R & S)
    2. –(P v Q)   ∴ R & S

23. 1. (P v Q) v (R & S)
    2. –(R & S)   ∴ P v Q

24. 1. ([A v B] v C) v D
    2. –D   ∴ (A v B) v C

25. 1. ([A v B] v C) v D
    2. –D
    3. –C   ∴ A v B

26. 1. ([A v B]v C) v D
    2. –D
    3. –C
    4. –A   ∴ B

HS (Hypothetical Syllogism)

27. 1. P → Q
    2. Q → R   ∴ P → R

28. 1. P → Q
    2. Q → R
    3. R → S   ∴ P → S

29. 1. (P & Q) → R
    2. R → S   ∴ (P & Q) → S

30. 1. (P & Q) → (R v S)
    2. (R v S) → T ∴ (P & Q) → T

31. 1. (P & Q) → R
    2. R → S
    3. S → (T v U) ∴ (P & Q) → (T v U)

32. 1. (C v Q) → −A
    2. −A → (R & K)
    3. (R & K) → Y ∴ (C v Q) → Y

Add (Addition)

33. 1. P   ∴ P v Q

34. 1. P & Q   ∴ (P & Q) v R

35. 1. P v Q   ∴ (P v Q) v R

36. 1. −P   ∴ −P v Q

37. 1. P & Q   ∴ (P & −Q) v R

38. 1. P   ∴ (P v Q) v R

Simp (Simplification)

39. 1. P & Q   ∴ P

40. 1. P & Q   ∴ Q

41. 1. R & S   ∴ R

42. 1. R & S   ∴ S

43. 1. (P & Q) & R ∴ R

44. 1. (P & Q) & R   ∴ P & Q

45. 1. (P & Q) & (R & S)   ∴ R

46. 1. (P & Q) & (R v S)
    2. Q → T   ∴ R v S

47. 1. (P & Q) & (R v S)
    2. Q → T   ∴ P

Conj (Conjunction)

48. 1. P
2. Q   ∴ P & Q

49. 1. P
2. Q   ∴ Q & P

50. 1. R
2. S   ∴ R & S

51. 1. P v Q
2. T   ∴ (P v Q) & T

52. 1. –P
2. Q & R   ∴ –P & (Q & R)

53. 1. –P
2. –Q & R   ∴ –P & (–Q & R)

54. 1. –P
2. –(Q & R)   ∴ –P & –(Q & R)

55. 1. P v Q
2. R & S
3. S → T   ∴ (P v Q) & ([R & S] & [S → T])

CD (Constructive Dilemma)

56. 1. $(P \rightarrow Q) \& (R \rightarrow S)$
    2. $P \lor R$ $\therefore Q \lor S$

57. 1. $(Q \rightarrow P) \& (S \rightarrow R)$
    2. $Q \lor S$ $\therefore P \lor R$

58. 1. $([A \& B] \rightarrow Q) \& (R \rightarrow S)$
    2. $(A \& B) \lor R$ $\therefore Q \lor S$

59. 1. $([A \lor B] \rightarrow Q) \& ([C \& D] \rightarrow S)$
    2. $(A \lor B) \lor (C \& D)$ $\therefore Q \lor S$

60. 1. $([[A \lor B] \& C] \rightarrow Q) \& ([D \& E] \rightarrow S)$
    2. $([A \lor B] \& C) \lor (D \& E)$ $\therefore Q \lor S$

61. 1. $(P \rightarrow Q) \& (R \rightarrow S)$
    2. $P \lor R$
    3. $(Q \rightarrow T) \& (S \rightarrow U)$ $\therefore T \lor U$

62. 1. $([A \leftrightarrow B] \rightarrow Q) \& (R \rightarrow S)$
    2. $R \lor (A \leftrightarrow B)$ $\therefore Q \lor S$

63. 1. $([A \leftrightarrow B] \rightarrow Q) \& (R \rightarrow S)$
    2. $R \lor (A \leftrightarrow B)$
    3. $(Q \rightarrow T) \& (S \rightarrow U)$ $\therefore T \lor U$

64. 1. $([A \leftrightarrow B] \rightarrow Q) \& (R \rightarrow S)$
    2. $R \lor (A \leftrightarrow B)$
    3. $(Q \rightarrow T) \& (S \rightarrow U)$
    4. $(T \rightarrow W) \& (U \rightarrow [X \& Y])$ $\therefore W \lor (X \& Y)$

Multi-rule Proofs

65. 1. P → Q
2. P v R
3. −R   ∴ Q

66. 1. P & Q
2. Q → R   ∴ R

67. 1. P & −Q
2. R → Q   ∴ −R

68. 1. P v Q
2. Q → R
3. P → (S v T)
4. −R   ∴ S v T

69. 1. P → Q
2. Q → (R v S)
3. −S & P   ∴ R

70. 1. ([A & B] → Q) & ([C v D] → S)
2. A & B
3. C   ∴ Q & S

71. 1. (A → Q) & ([(C v D) → E] → S)
2. A & B
3. D   ∴ Q v S

72. 1. P → Q
2. R → S
3. P
4. R   ∴ Q & S

73. 1. P → Q
2. P   ∴ Q v R

74. 1. P → (Q & R)
2. P   ∴ Q

75. 1. P → Q
2. P   ∴ P & Q

76. 1. P → Q
2. R → S
3. P   ∴ Q v S

CHAPTER 9

Advanced Proof Techniques: Conditional Proof and Indirect Proof

In this chapter we will learn two advanced proof techniques: conditional proof and indirect proof (also called *reductio ad absurdum*).

Conditional proof allows us to construct new implication statements by assuming a statement to be true and then demonstrating what other statements would be entailed by its truth. Indirect proof is a special variety of conditional proof in which we assume a statement to be true but then derive a contradiction from that assumption. Because we know contradictions cannot be true, if we derive a contradiction from assuming a statement is true, then we know that the statement must be false.

Both of these techniques involve producing a sub-proof. A sub-proof is a proof that resides within a larger, main proof. Sub-proofs are indented and marked off from the main proof with vertical bars to indicate that the steps in the sub-proof cannot be used in the main proof. Only the result of a sub-proof can be used in the main proof. We will start by learning how to construct a conditional proof and then examine indirect proof afterwards.

9.1 Conditional Proof

Conditional Proof (CP)

$$P$$
$$...$$
$$Q$$
$$\therefore P \rightarrow Q$$

As was just noted, conditional proof is an advanced proof technique that allows us to create new implication statements through a sub-proof by seeing what statements are entailed by an assumption. We engage in this kind of thinking quite often. In natural language, we note the hypothetical nature of such reasoning with phrases such as "what would happen if ..." or "if X were true, then what would follow?"

Let's start with a natural language example: Yoda will want to either cuddle in the recliner or go for a walk. But if it's raining, then she won't want to go for a walk. So, if it's raining, she'll want to cuddle in the recliner.

At first glance, this reasoning makes sense. We will symbolize this argument as follows:

R = "It is raining."
W = "Yoda wants to go for a walk."
C = "Yoda wants to cuddle in the recliner."
1. R → −W
2. W v C   ∴ R → C

By looking at the symbolized argument, you can see that if R is true, then we can apply DS to produce the desired conclusion. However, the premises do not provide R; our natural language example did not assert that it actually *was* raining, it just stated what would be true if it *were* raining. This is an instance where conditional proof may be applied.

1. $R \rightarrow -W$
2. $W \lor C$ $\therefore R \rightarrow C$
   | 3. R   CPA
   | 4. $-W$ 1, 3, MP
   | 5. C   2, 4, DS
6. $R \rightarrow C$ 3–5, CP

You will notice three new features in this proof that have not been used so far in this text: (1) line 3 is marked "CPA," (2) lines 3–5 are indented and are marked off with a line, and (3) line 6 is marked "CP." These features identify a conditional proof is being used. "CPA" means "conditional proof assumption." We begin every conditional proof by making an assumption and marking it as "CPA." We offset the lines of a conditional proof, starting with the assumption and ending the offset with the last line before we "discharge" the conditional proof by returning to a normal line (i.e., a line that is not offset and is not marked with a vertical bar). Lastly, "CP" means "conditional proof"; we note which line numbers are used and mark them.

Let's work through this example proof. In line 3 we assume R is true and mark it "CPA" to indicate this is our conditional proof assumption. We indent this line and mark it with a vertical bar to indicate that what we assert on this line was not already contained in the proof's premises. You can assume anything is true at the start of a conditional proof, but not all assumptions will actually help you complete the proof. When producing a conditional proof, you should have a clear objective in mind, and begin with an assumption that will help you achieve that objective. In this case, the objective is the implication statement (R → C), and CP will get that statement if we assume the antecedent, R (and get to C). So only by assuming R can CP get us to that objective.

Line 4 is also offset and marked with a vertical bar to show that we are still completing the conditional proof. We complete line 4 (and all subsequent lines) in the way we normally complete lines in a proof, i.e., indicating which previous line(s) and which rule of inference or logical equivalent we are applying. In this case, we apply MP to lines 1 and 3 to get −W. After we have introduced a conditional proof assumption, we are allowed to use it like any other preceding line in the proof *within* (and only within) the conditional proof for which we introduced it. In line 5, we get C by applying DS to lines 2 and 4.

On line 5 we have achieved this conditional proof's objective, which was to show that if R is true then C will be true as well. We are now in a position to end our conditional proof. We do that by exiting the proof in line 6 and writing our new implication statement R → C. This new implication statement formally captures what we showed in the intervening lines. Line 6 is not part of the conditional proof because it does not rest on an assumption. We show that a conditional proof was used to get line 6 by marking all of the lines used in the conditional proof (no matter how many lines it took) and writing "CP" beside it. Given that this is all we were trying to prove in this case, the proof is complete on line 6. A vertical line is drawn showing the extent of the sub-derivation.

Let's look at another example:

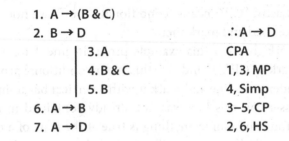

1. A → (B & C)
2. B → D   ∴ A → D
   3. A   CPA
   4. B & C   1, 3, MP
   5. B   4, Simp
6. A → B   3–5, CP
7. A → D   2, 6, HS

Lines 3–5 are a conditional proof that yield a new implication statement on line 6, which is then used along with other statements to derive the argument's conclusion. Using conditional proof, we have managed to show that if A is true, then D will be true as well. As you should be able to tell from these examples, conditional proof is a powerful technique.

9.2 Indirect Proof (*Reductio ad Absurdum*)

Indirect Proof (IP)

P   **or**   −P
...
Q & −Q   Q & −Q
∴ −P   ∴ P

Indirect proof is similar to conditional proof, but instead of deriving an implication statement it allows us to show that a statement is true or false, even when it is not directly asserted to be so in an argument's premises. This proof technique is also frequently called "*reductio ad absurdum*," which is Latin for "reduction to absurdity." This technique has a long history of use in philosophy. It is used to show that a statement must be true because its falsity is absurd, rather than by providing independent evidence that the statement is true. Indirect proof can be used to derive a conclusion that could not otherwise be derived, and it can also be used in intermediate steps of a proof.

Here is a natural language example of this technique: "if the Earth were flat, then people would fall off of it if they reached a certain point. Because people do not fall off the Earth, then the Earth must not be flat."

When this technique is used in statement logic, the absurdity in question is a contradiction. Because we know that the same statement cannot be true and false at the same time, if any assertion would result in a contradiction, then we know that the assertion must be false.

An indirect proof is written in a way very similar to how a conditional proof is written. We mark the lines involved in an indirect proof and indent them. We mark the assumption that begins the indirect proof with "IPA" which stands for "indirect proof assumption." When we close the indirect proof, we return to the main line (i.e., a non-intended line), record all the lines of the indirect proof, and write "IP" for "indirect proof."

Here is an example to demonstrate how indirect proof functions:

```
   1. -A → -B
   2. B                    ∴ A
      │ 3. -A              IPA
      │ 4. -B              1, 3, MP
      │ 5. B & -B          2, 4, Conj
   6. A                    3-5, IP
```

On line 3 we assume that −A is true. We make this assumption because
−A contradicts our desired conclusion A. Our objective in this proof is
to show that A must be true because if −A is true a contradiction will
result. On line 4 we apply MP to lines 1 and 3 and derive −B. On line
5 we demonstrate that our assumption −A results in B & −B. Because
a statement and its negation cannot both be true at the same time, we
know that our assumption must in fact be false. If −A is false, then A
is true, which we show on line 6 by closing the indirect proof (by not
indenting this line or marking it with a vertical bar), noting the lines
involved in the sub-proof, and marking it "IP."[13]

Let's look at two other examples of how we can use indirect proof:

```
   1. (P v Q) → R           ∴ -(P & -R)
      │ 2. P & -R           IPA
      │ 3. P                2, Simp
      │ 4. P v Q            3, Add
      │ 5. R                1, 4, MP
      │ 6. -R               2, Simp
      │ 7. R & -R           5, 6, Conj
   8. -(P & -R)             2-7, IP
```

This example is more complex than our first one. We begin our indirect
proof by assuming that the conclusion is false on line 2. Lines 3 through
7 apply rules we are already familiar with, aiming for, and getting to, a
contradiction on line 7. Since the negation of this assumption is our conclusion, we've completed our proof. We show this on line 8 by asserting
that the conclusion is true based on the indirect proof offered on lines 2-7.

---

13. As you will see in the next chapter, this proof can also be solved using a
logical equivalent called "double negation" and an application of MT.

In this last example, we'll use indirect proof to prove an intermediate line in the proof rather than the main conclusion.

1.	$-A \rightarrow -B$	
2.	B	
3.	$A \rightarrow C$	
4.	$C \rightarrow D$	$\therefore D$
5.	$A \rightarrow D$	3, 4, HS
6.	$-A$	IPA
7.	$-B$	1, 6, MP
8.	$B \& -B$	2, 7, Conj
9.	A	6–8, IP
10.	D	5, 9, MP

In this example, we ultimately aim to prove that D is true. We can see from looking at the premises that we will need to assert C to assert D (line 4), and to assert C we will need to assert A (line 3). We assert A, as we did in the first example, by using indirect proof. This time our indirect proof appears on lines 6–8. As this example demonstrates, indirect proof can be used at any stage of an argument where we have enough information to show that a statement must be true because its falsity would result in a contradiction.

When engaging with complex proofs, keep conditional proof and indirect proof in mind as advanced techniques that will allow you to derive lines you may not otherwise be able to derive. It is normally worth seeing if there are ways of solving the proof using only the rules of inference and logical equivalents first. If you see that an additional implication statement is required but you cannot create it using the rules of inference and logical equivalents, then try to use a conditional proof instead. If you need to prove a statement is true and realize that its falsity would result in a contradiction because of the other statements in the argument, then try to use an indirect proof for that purpose.

9.3 Multiple Sub-Proofs

Sometimes two (or more) of these techniques are needed, one inside the other. We may have as many sub-proofs as are necessary to complete our proof, and we can create as many sub-proofs as we need layered inside of other sub-proofs. However, we must always follow the rules for sub-proofs introduced earlier, namely that we can only use the lines in a sub-proof within that sub-proof, though we may use the result of a sub-proof in the next layer up. That means if we only have one sub-proof, we may use the result of it in the main proof, but if we have a sub-proof within another sub-proof, then we can only use the result of the one sub-proof in the other sub-proof (which is one layer up). For example:

$$1.\ P \& Q \quad \therefore P \to (Q \to P)$$

2. P		CPA
3. Q		CPA
4. P		1, Simp
5. Q → P		3–4, CP
6. P → (Q → P)		2–5, CP

In this example, we can only use lines 3–4 to produce a result (line 5) to be used in the sub-proof one layer up (which starts on line 2 and ends on line 5). We may then use what is in the sub-proof that ends on line 5 in the main proof, which ends on line 6.

Consider a regular proof (i.e., not a sub-proof) to be layer 1. A sub-proof (lines 2–5 in this example) are layer 2. A sub-proof within a sub-proof is another layer down (e.g., lines 3–4 are layer 3 in this example), and so on. As a rule, only the final result of a sub-proof may be used one layer up. No other part of the sub-proof may be used anywhere else in the proof, and the result of a sub-proof may never be used anywhere but on the next layer up.

Now consider the following three items. Are they correct?

1. P & Q ∴ P → (Q → P)
| 2. P   1, Simp
| | 3. Q   CPA
| | 4. P   1, Simp
| 5. Q → P   3–4, CP
6. P → (Q → P)   2–5, CP

This is incorrect. Line 2 is the assumption for the conditional proof on lines 2–5, so it must be marked CPA.

1. P & (P → Q) ∴ Q
| 2. P   CPA
| 3. (P → Q)   1, Simp
| 4. Q   2, 3, MP
5. P → Q   2–4, CP
6. P   1, Simp
7. Q   5, 6, MP

1. P & (P → Q) ∴ Q
| 2. P   IPA
| 3. P → Q   1, Simp
| 4. Q   2, 3, MP

The answers are that the upper proof is correct, but the lower proof is incorrect. In the upper proof, every step is a correct use of the rule. But look at it carefully: it's inelegant to the point of stupidity. That whole CP section is unnecessary. The whole thing could have been done with what two Simps and a MP.

The lower proof is incorrect. The last step of this item is indeed the logical object that was supposed to be proven. But this does not prove it: that object must be outside any assumption area—that is, without any vertical line preceding it. Maybe, then, you'd be tempted to substitute the following (by adding an additional step):

1. $P \& (P \rightarrow Q)$ $\therefore Q$
  | 2. P   IPA
  | 3. $P \rightarrow Q$ 1, Simp
  | 4. Q   2, 3, MP
5. Q   4, R

But step 5 is incorrect. As mentioned above, the steps in a sub-proof cannot be used in the main proof. Only the result of a whole sub-proof can be used in the main proof—or, for that matter, in any other sub-proof that is not inside that whole sub-proof.

If this is confusing to you, think of that vertical line (in this case, to the left of steps 2, 3, and 4) as a one-way justification gate. Anything to the right of that line can be justified by what's to the right of that line as well, or through that "gate" by what's to the left of it (in this case, step 1). But what's to the left of it (e.g., step 5) cannot be justified by what's to the right of it.

Here's an ordinary-language example that illustrates the sort of mistake we're talking about.

SAL: Fred might not get here till after six. And he'll want dinner after he gets here.

AL: So?

SAL: | *SUPPOSE* Fred gets here after six. *(This is the assumption for conditional proof: the line we mark CPA)*
       | He'll want dinner after six.
       | Dinner will take an hour, and the movie begins at 6:30.
       | So we'll be too late to get to the movie.

SO: IF Fred gets here after six, THEN we'll be too late to get to the movie. *(This is the conditional statement which is the result of the reasoning in the sub-derivation—the line we mark CP.)*

AL: Are you saying that we'll be too late for the movie? *(Here's that mistake—justifying [by R] a line inside the subderivation for the conditional proof.)*

SAL: No—I'm saying that IF he gets here after six, THEN we'll be too late to get to the movie.

9.4 Practice Questions

Conditional Proof
Use conditional proof to solve the following practice questions.

1. 1. P → –Q
   2. Q v R   ∴ P → R

2. 1. (P v Q) → –R
   2. R v –S   ∴ (P v Q) → –S

3. 1. P → (Q & R)
   2. R → T   ∴ P → T

4. 1. P → Q
   2. R → S   ∴ (P v R) → (Q v S)

5. 1. Q → R
   2. R → S   ∴ (P → Q) → (P → S)

6. 1. P → –Q
   2. R v S
   3. S → Q   ∴ P → R

7. 1. P → –Q
   2. Q v R   ∴ P → (–Q & R)

Indirect Proof
Use indirect proof to answer the following practice questions. Note: these proofs can be accomplished without using indirect proof, but use it anyway.

8. 1. P → Q
   2. Q → –P   ∴ –P

9. 1. P v Q
   2. Q → P   ∴ P

10. 1. –(R v S)
   2. P → R
   3. Q → S   ∴ –(P v Q)

11. 1. (P v Q) → –P   ∴ –P

12. 1. P → (Q & –Q)   ∴ –P

Multiple Sub-Proofs
Use multiple sub-proofs to answer the following practice questions, even if you can produce a proof for them without using multiple sub-proofs.

13. 1. P → Q
   2. Q → R v S
   3. Q → –R   ∴ P → S

14. 1. Q → –R
   2. R v (P v S)
   3. –P v –Q   ∴ Q → S

CHAPTER 10

Logical Equivalents and Complex Proofs

10.1 Logical Equivalents
10.2 Using Logical Equivalents
10.3 Practice Questions

In chapter 8 we introduced proofs, examined rules of inference, and briefly discussed logical equivalents. Logical equivalents are similar to rules of inference insofar as they are valid "moves" you can make in a proof. There is a difference between rules of inference and logical equivalents. When we apply a rule of inference, we are indicating that a new inference (or act of reasoning) has been conducted, and we are moving step by step towards the desired conclusion. However, when we apply a logical equivalent, we are simply restating information that we already have (just as we can rephrase a statement in English, or other natural language) into a different statement with the same meaning using synonyms or different phrases. Logical equivalents can be used to restate formulas in a proof in a way that allows us to apply rules of inference in new and interesting ways. This can help us move towards our desired conclusion in a proof.

10.1 Logical Equivalents

There are ten logical equivalents that we will learn. Here is a table with the ten logical equivalents:

Logical Equivalent (shorthand symbols)	Equivalent function (in symbolic form)
Double negation (DN)	$P \equiv --P$
Transposition (Trans)	$P \to Q \equiv -Q \to -P$
Material Implication (MI)	$P \to Q \equiv -P \lor Q$
De Morgan's Rule (DM)	$-(P \& Q) \equiv -P \lor -Q$ $-(P \lor Q) \equiv -P \& -Q$
Tautology (Taut)	$P \equiv P \lor P$ $P \equiv P \& P$
Commutation (Comm)	$P \lor Q \equiv Q \lor P$ $P \& Q \equiv Q \& P$
Association (Assoc)	$P \lor (Q \lor R) \equiv (P \lor Q) \lor R$ $P \& (Q \& R) \equiv (P \& Q) \& R$
Distribution (Dist)	$P \& (Q \lor R) \equiv (P \& Q) \lor (P \& R)$ $P \lor (Q \& R) \equiv (P \lor Q) \& (P \lor R)$
Material Equivalence (ME)	$(P \leftrightarrow Q) \equiv (P \to Q) \& (Q \to P)$ $(P \leftrightarrow Q) \equiv (P \& Q) \lor (-P \& -Q)$
Exportation (Exp)	$(P \& Q) \to R \equiv P \to (Q \to R)$

1. Logical equivalents are expressed differently than the rules of inference in symbolic form. For each equivalent, two expressions are connected by the logical equivalency symbol ($\equiv$) as seen on the table. In a proof, whenever you encounter one of the expressions shown in the table, you may replace it with the other logically equivalent expression. The logical equivalency symbol can be read as "is identical to" or "may be substituted with."

2. Logically equivalent expressions may be substituted anywhere they occur in a proof, even to a logical unit that is only part of a larger complex statement. By contrast, rules of inference apply to entire lines of a proof, i.e., you cannot apply a rule of inference to any part of an expression, but only to expressions as a whole.

3. You can see that all of the expressions joined by $\equiv$ on the table are logically equivalent by constructing a truth table for each

equivalent expression. For the sake of economy, these truth tables will not be provided in this chapter.[14]

4. One other note on the table and examples is that although simple statements are used in the expressions, complex statements may be used in their place, just as was the case with the rules of inference introduced in chapter 8.

10.2 Using Logical Equivalents

We have now examined all of the rules of inference and logical equivalents that will be introduced in this book. Let us examine some quick examples of when logical equivalents can be used in a proof and consider some advice on how to approach difficult proofs.

1.	P → −(Q v R)	
2.	Q v R	∴ −P
3.	(Q v R)	2, DN
4.	−P	1, 3, MT

Here we see an example where DN (double negation) can be used together with MT to easily solve this proof. This proof could also be solved using an indirect proof, but that would take more lines than solving it with double negation takes.

Keep in mind that you can combine the rules and equivalents to set each other up. For example, ME (Material Equivalence) can be used to turn a biconditional into a conjoined set of implication statements. You can simplify the conjunction to isolate one of those statements, and then apply MP or MT to it:

1.	P ↔ Q	
2.	P	∴ Q
3.	(P → Q) & (Q → P)	1, ME
4.	P → Q	3, Simp
5.	Q	2, 4, MP

---

14. More detailed explanations of each equivalent are available on the companion website to this book.

In the following example, (Q v P) replaces its Commutation equivalent, (P v Q), inside the larger expression (Q v P) → S.

1. P v Q
2. (Q v P) → S   ∴ S
3. (P v Q) → S   2, Comm
4. S   1, 3, MP

There are many other such combinations that can be produced by combining the rules of inference and the logical equivalents. Rather than listing all of those combinations here, let us instead turn to the practice questions that will require you to discover and apply these combinations. When approaching a proof you should first examine the premises and conclusion and consider what strategy to adopt in trying to solve it. Look to see if the conclusion is contained somewhere in the premises. If it is not, look for the component parts of the conclusion in the premises and think about what rules of inference or logical equivalents you could use to produce the desired conclusion. If some creativity is required in producing the desired conclusion, use the forward- and backward-looking approaches to the proof described in section 8.5. In general, try looking for how the rules of inference can be applied first, and then consider how you may restate one or more parts of the argument using logical equivalences afterwards. Sometimes applying a logical equivalence will make it possible to apply a rule of inference you otherwise could not apply or reduce the number of lines the proof will take to complete.

If a proof strategy is not apparent after reviewing the argument's component parts, simply experimenting with the "moves" you can see will reveal other possibilities to you, so it can be worth producing a first rough version of a proof if you aren't sure where you will end up.

We have now reached the end of our introduction to formal logic! Although formal logic can be used to analyze very complicated arguments, like many complex systems it is ultimately composed of many simple parts working together. At this point you have learned all of those simple parts. You now have the skills required to produce a proof for any valid argument in statement logic, and to demonstrate the validity or invalidity of any argument in statement logic using truth tables.[15]

10.3 Practice Questions

Answer the following practice proofs by using the rules of inference and/or logical equivalences.

1.   1. –(P & Q)
       2. Q   ∴ –P

2.   1. –(P v Q)
       2. –Q → R   ∴ R

3.   1. P → Q
       2. Q → R   ∴ R → P

4.   1. P → Q
       2. –P → –R   ∴ –Q → –R

5.   1. P ↔ Q
       2. Q   ∴ P

6.   1. P & Q
       2. Q → R   ∴ Q v Q

7.   1. (P & Q) & R
       2. R → S & (T & U)   ∴ (S & T) & U

8.   1. P
       2. Q v –R
       3. –R → –P   ∴ Q

---

15. For a short glimpse at the field of symbolic deductive logic that's often studied next, look at the supplemental web material.

9. 1. P
2. P → (Q → R)
3. Q   ∴ R

10. 1. P ↔ Q
2. Q → R   ∴ P → R

11. 1. –(P v Q)
2. R → Q   ∴ –R

12. 1. P
2. –P v Q   ∴ Q

13. 1. (P & Q) → R
2. (Q → R) → S   ∴ P → S

14. 1. P v (Q & S)
2. P → R
3. –S   ∴ R

15. 1. –(P v Q)
2. Q v R
3. R → S   ∴ S v T

16. 1. P & Q
2. –Q v –R
3. –S → –P   ∴ S & –R

17. 1. P & (Q v R)
2. (P & Q) → S
3. (P & R) → T   ∴ S v T

The following questions can be solved using conditional proof or indirect proof in addition to logical equivalences.

18. 1. $P \rightarrow Q$
2. $Q \leftrightarrow R$ $\therefore P \rightarrow R$

19. 1. $P \rightarrow Q$
2. $Q \leftrightarrow R$ $\therefore -R \rightarrow -P$

20. 1. P
2. $-Q \vee R$ $\therefore Q \rightarrow (R \vee T)$

21. 1. $P \leftrightarrow (Q \,\&\, R)$ $\therefore P \rightarrow R$

From the Publisher

A name never says it all, but the word "Broadview" expresses
a good deal of the philosophy behind our company. We are
open to a broad range of academic approaches and political
viewpoints. We pay attention to the broad impact book
publishing and book printing has in the wider world; for
some years now we have used 100% recycled paper for most
titles. Our publishing program is internationally oriented and
broad-ranging. Our individual titles often appeal to a broad
readership too; many are of interest as much to general readers
as to academics and students.

Founded in 1985, Broadview remains a fully independent
company owned by its shareholders—not an imprint or
subsidiary of a larger multinational.

To order our books or obtain up-to-date information,
please visit broadviewpress.com.

broadview press
www.broadviewpress.com

Rules for Truth Table Formation (Chapter 2)

1. Identify all of the statements in the argument.
2. Create a header row. Starting at the left, create a column for each simple statement in the argument.
3. Add columns for each complex statement in the argument.
4. Label each premise and conclusion at the top of your truth table.
5. Determine the number of rows your table will require. A truth table requires 2^n rows in addition to the header row. n equals the number of simple statements in the argument.
6. Enter the truth values in the cells in each column that represents a simple statement.
7. Enter the truth values in the cells in each column that represents a complex statement.

Steps for utilizing the Long Truth Table Method (Chapter 5)

1. Construct a truth table that fully diagrams the argument to be tested for validity. (Steps 1–7 of "Rules" above)
2. Identify each row where the conclusion is false.
3. Read across each row where the conclusion is false to check the truth of the premises. If you find at least one row where the conclusion is false and all of the premises are true, then the argument is invalid. If you do not find such a row, then the argument is valid.

Steps for Using the Short Truth Table Method (Chapter 6)

1. Create the header row for a truth table that represents the argument (Steps 1–4 of "Rules" above); then add a single row under the header row.
2. Set the argument's conclusion to false.
3. Begin setting premises to true, while avoiding contradictions if possible.
4. If you created a row where the premises are true and the conclusion false without contradiction, the argument is invalid. If you couldn't make such a row but there's another way for the conclusion to be false, create this new row and repeat steps 2–4. If there's no way to make the conclusion false and the premises true without contradiction, the argument is valid.